Where the Potomac Begins

Where the Potomac Begins

A History of the
North Branch Valley

GILBERT GUDE

Seven Locks Press
Publishers
Cabin John, Md./Washington, D.C.

Library of Congress Cataloging in Publication Data

Gude, Gilbert, 1923–
    Where the Potomac begins.

    Bibliography: p.
    Includes index.
    1. Potomac River Valley—History.   2. Potomac River
Valley—Industries.   3. Potomac River, North Branch
(W. Va. and Md.)   I. Title.
F187.P8G76   975.2   84-14120
ISBN 0-932020-32-1

Manufactured in the United States of America

Designed by Chuck Myers

Typography and composition by Options Type Group,
Takoma Park, Maryland

Printed by the Maple Press Company, York, Pennsylvania

First edition, December 1984

SEVEN LOCKS PRESS
Publishers
P.O. Box 72   Cabin John, Maryland 20818
301-320-2130

To Jane

Acknowledgments

Sincere thanks to several of the citizens of Kempton, Maryland, and Elk Garden, West Virginia. In Kempton, Gladys Corbin, her daughters Wanda Corbin and Maxine Corbin Repetsky, and Twila and Elmer Clark have been unfailingly gracious in their patience, hospitality, and friendship. Roy Wiseman and former mayors Patricia Groppleman and Jessie Reel have given generously of their time to help me tell as accurately as possible the story of Elk Garden in past and present times.

My deep appreciation also to those who have given me particular insights into technical and historical matters, as well as to those who have made valuable suggestions, criticisms, and comments during the course of my writing: Allen F. Agnew, Earle Palmer Brown, William E. Davies, George Danko, Irene Anne Ferrar, Charles A. Goodrum, Sharon K. Green, Adrienne A. Gude, Sharon Gude, Raymond W. Hicks, A. A. Hoehling, John R. Justus, Sergius H. Mamay, Roy H. Millenson, John Pearce, Jane Powers, Dana J. Pratt, Jennings Randolph, Mona Ridder, Orlando Ridout V, James Sayler, Anne Schoen, Robert E. Trumbule, Robert A. Wall, Donna Ware, and John Alexander Williams.

Picture Credits

Map by Joseph Wiedel and Margarita Tadilla, 2.
Photographs by Claire Flanders, 4, 5, 11, 98, 99, 110, 111, 134, 138, 146, 153.
Photograph by Chip Clark, 7; courtesy the Museum of National History, the Smithsonian Institution.
Archives, Library of Congress, 30, 34, 35, 37, 38, 116.
Cartoon from *Judge*, October 29, 1904, 37.
Photographer unknown, courtesy Ray Hicks, 46–47, 50, 103, 104, 108, 109.
Photographs by John Vachon, 47 bottom, 48, 64, 68, 70, 80–94, FSA collection, Library of Congress.
Photograph by West Virginia Photo Co., Parsons, West Va., 76.

The lines on page 153 are from *Out of the Bog and Other Poems* by Dr. Harold Strong Gulliver, Sr. Copyright 1938 by Henry Harrison. By permission.

Foreword

Like many of the dedicated visionaries who established
the Republic more than two centuries ago, the Potomac
traces its origins to humble beginnings. The sweep of
the mature river as it flows past Washington toward the
Chesapeake Bay belies its source, a small spring on a
West Virginia mountaintop. From there it grows from
a trickle, to a branch, to a coursing river. At Harpers
Ferry it absorbs the Shenandoah in a scene that Thomas
Jefferson called worth a trip across the Atlantic. Finally
it becomes the serene Potomac that Washington and the
nation know so well.

The beginnings of the Potomac are less well known.
The area is relatively remote. Its coal mining towns, its
lumber camps, and its railroad junctions have known
good times and bad, boom and bust. The people of this
sparsely populated region are closely associated with the
land and the river and draw their strength from them.

The upper reaches of the Potomac in Western Maryland and West Virginia were known to George Washington, who, as a young surveyor and later as an en-
trepreneur, dreamed of building a canal across the mountains to the Ohio River. Abraham Lincoln's mother,
Nancy Hanks, was born nearby. The Baltimore and
Ohio Railroad penetrated the area more than 150 years
ago on its westward sweep to open new areas of the country to commerce.

It was into this region rich in history that Gilbert Gude
traveled. As a member of Congress from Maryland and
later as director of the Congressional Research Service,

he has examined with clarity and perception the land
and its people. From the creation of coal deposits in
prehistoric centuries to the current threat of acid rain,
he has traced the geology, the history, and the commerce
of the Upper Potomac region, always relating them to
the people who live there.

West Virginia has been called "the mother of rivers."
It is proud to have given birth to the Potomac and to
be the source of this great national waterway. In *Where
the Potomac Begins* Gilbert Gude enhances not only our
knowledge but our appreciation of this unique national
treasure.

Jennings Randolph
United States Senator
West Virginia

Washington
May 23, 1984

Contents

Where the Potomac Begins

A History of the North Branch Valley

*The land, the coal, and the people — especially
the people of Kempton, Maryland,
and Elk Garden, West Virginia.*

Author's Preface

To better understand the Potomac, its valley, and its people, I decided in the middle 1970s to travel the almost four-hundred mile length of the river, from its first spring in the West Virginia mountains to its confluence with the Chesapeake Bay. My plan was to build upon my experiences in a decade of excursions—to the Fairfax Stone, Catoctin, Sharpsburg, Harpers Ferry, Stratford, St. Mary's City, Point Look Out, and also to Lonaconing, Little Orleans, Charles Town, Leesburg, Seneca, and Port Tobacco, the many lesser known towns and places in between. Fortunately, in August 1975 Congress had a month's recess, so the journey didn't have to be a marathon. I had plenty of time to build an empathy with the people who live along the river and to learn the Potomac in their terms of reference, which I very much wanted to do. It was then that I came to have something larger than a tourist's understanding of the North Branch Valley, encompassing not only its history and people, but also its future and its relevance to many critical concerns of society today.

For the first fifty miles from the Fairfax Stone this region is a Brigadoon world—a misty green valley of Allegheny coal country, lumber towns, company coal towns, and ghost towns. This is a piece of Appalachia, and it is markedly different from the foothills and coastal plains of the east. Here, at its beginning, the river runs vigorously through many small rapids and falls, whereas at its end it flows leisurely with the tides. The rolling landscape of the headlands seems far removed, even estranged, from both the Piedmont, with its great Washington metropolis, and the Tidewater culture of southern Maryland and Virginia's northern neck. Yet, in one striking particular, the North Branch Valley and the Tidewater region are sadly alike. The more recent exploitation of the timber and fossil-fuel extractive industries of the Allegheny plateau is only a different manifestation of the same economic forces that in colonial times depleted the soil of the lowlands. At its beginning and at its end, the Potomac is drawn together by a common history of environmental abuse.

Like any congressman, I'd been a careful observer and interpreter of my constituencies, so I was comfortable studying the small valley and talking with its inhabitants. In the tiny village of Kempton, the "first" town in Maryland, where the Potomac is only several miles from the Fairfax Stone, I came to know the miners, former miners, miners' widows, and their children and grandchildren who live in the last nine of the company houses. In nearby Oakland I found the former principal of Kempton High and his wife, and in Dundalk, near Baltimore, one of the former union presidents.

A few miles downstream from Kempton, at more sophisticated Elk Garden, West Virginia, I met town officials and former miners, including one engaging elderly gentleman who, as a young telegraph operator, had provided communication from the mouth of the Elk Garden mine after the terrible explosion of 1911 that killed several dozen men, some of them fathers and their sons. All told, the reminiscences of these mining people gave me a full, rich picture of life in the North Branch Valley over the past half century. They talked plainly, most often matter-of-factly, and in an idiom shy of metaphor—in poignant counterpoint, I thought, to the soaring optimism and flamboyant style of the industrialists of the development decades of the turn of the century.

But to truly understand the Upper Potomac Valley, I found that it was not enough to meet the people who live there now or to familiarize myself with the region's history since 1900. Indeed, I had to go back as far as the paleobiologists and geologists could take me, and ultimately even what they could tell me was not enough. I found that, as precise as the scientists were in describing the coal-formation epochs, the prehistory of the Upper North Branch Valley could be fully appreciated only through the inspired insights of the biblical psalmists and prophetic poets.

During the last half of the nineteenth century, when the timber and coal of this Upper Potomac Valley were being developed, Walt Whitman was writing the poetry for *Leaves of Grass*. In one poem, "Passage to India," he gives us a vision of the world when it was young. His vision is invested with the unrestrained enthusiasm that marked industrial development during those decades, and the poem itself tends to affirm a popular notion of his day—that from the very beginning, with the creation of coal, indeed with the creation of all man's material world, this industrial development had been preordained. In a comment published in the 1892 edition of *Leaves of Grass*, he was explicit:

> While I cannot understand it or argue it out, I fully believe in a clue and purpose in Nature, entire and several; and that invisible spiritual results, just as real and definite as the visible, eventuate all concrete life and all materialism, through Time.

Learning about the Upper Potomac has been, for me, a search for congruence among politics, history, science, literature, and poetry. What follows is a brief but faithful report of that search.

Gilbert Gude
June, 1984

PART ONE

Creation and Development

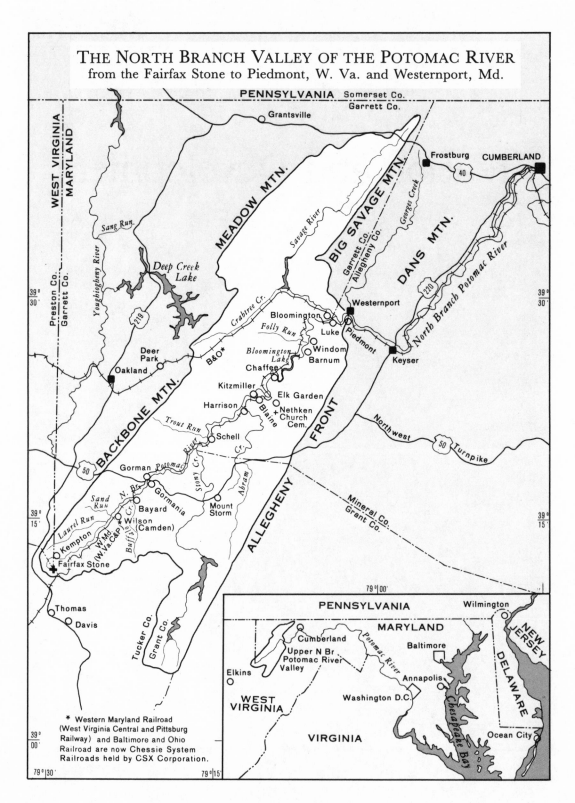

THE NORTH BRANCH VALLEY OF THE POTOMAC RIVER
from the Fairfax Stone to Piedmont, W. Va. and Westernport, Md.

* Western Maryland Railroad
(West Virginia Central and Pittsburg
Railway) and Baltimore and Ohio
Railroad are now Chessie System
Railroads held by CSX Corporation.

1

Coalmaker and Associates

O, vast Rondure, swimming
in space.
Cover'd all over with visible
power and beauty.
Alternate light and day,
and the teeming spiritual darkness;
Unspeakable, high procession of
sun and moon, and countless
stars above;
Below, the manifold grass and
waters, animals, mountains, trees;
With inscrutable purpose — some
hidden prophetic intention, . . .

—Walt Whitman
"Passage to India"[1]

The Potomac officially begins a few miles within the
Allegheny plateau at a West Virginia spring near a ridge
of the Great Backbone Mountain. Its source is marked
by a small monolith, a replica of the Fairfax Stone that
once defined the beginning point of the royal land grant
to Lord Fairfax;[2] the stone now marks Maryland's western and southern boundaries. From this site the growing river—here known as the North Branch or Main
Stem—flows northeasterly through a narrow and deepening valley. Fifty miles from the Fairfax Stone, at Piedmont and Westernport, it turns sharply to the east in
a dramatic break through the Allegheny Front, and here
the valley ends.

The North Branch Valley is a region of timber and
agriculture, underlaid by seams of coal. To the north

The author at the Fairfax Stone, replica of the marker placed in 1746 by surveyors employed by Thomas, the sixth Lord Fairfax, to fix the northwest corner of his estate as defined in his royal land grant. Since 1910 the marker has also served as the baseline for the western boundary of Maryland. From the spring (left rear) flows a quiet brook, gathering strength to become the great Potomac. Thirty-five miles to the stone's northeast, the river and the Chessie railroad make graceful turns at Kitzmiller, Maryland.

are the uplands of Maryland—grassy glades, woods, and cropland. To the south are the rugged ridges and valley farms of West Virginia. While part of the region is like a pastoral cosmos, some of the mined-out mountain slopes pucker like fruit skins from which all the richness has been sucked. Great pyramidal heaps of mine waste, or "gob," further testify to the decades of mining; scars and gouges in the land are the price paid for rough timbering and strip mining. Scattered ghost towns, small villages, farms, and mobile houses are now the homes for the people of the North Branch Valley.

Coal and man are the main actors in the history of the valley, and so, appropriately, the story of the Potomac headlands begins in the main period of coal creation, three million centuries ago. This is the Carboniferous epoch. A time of strange swamp animals, bizarre plants, and giant insects, it spans tens of thousands of centuries, including the end of the Mississippian, all of the Pennsylvanian, and the beginning of the Permian geologic periods. Even with geology charts we can barely comprehend its dimensions, with its immense conver-

sions and storage of solar energy and its vast corridors in time.

But visit the North Branch Valley on a midsummer day and one can feel the tug of this earlier age on the imagination. Here the headlands have the quality of a Cezanne painting. Sunlight, interspersed with shadows of the passing clouds, sweeps slowly over the landscape. The low mountains resemble long ovals, rectangles, and truncated pyramids. The pale greens of the pastures and crop fields—polygons and trapezoids—blend with the deeper shades of tree crops; with each breeze a choreography of greens unfolds, as leaves and needles of oak, poplar, gum, spruce, and pine radiate in wave after wave, creating pirouettes of olive, emerald, and malachite. All through the valley the small river makes its way with busy chattering sounds over stone and gravel, while a strong breeze stirring the foliage along the side of a forested mountain makes a simmering sound. The gossipy river and the glittering leaves seem to move and speak in concert. Millions of photocells wink in the sunlight, flashing chlorophyll as they build sugars from the breeze, the soft mist, and the sun. It is all of a piece. The long, low mountains, the clouds, the farms, and the river seem linked to the land, and the effect is hypnotic. Irresistibly, the mind is drawn as if through a time warp to a period three million centuries ago.

A strong breeze stirs the grasslike leaves of strange great Carboniferous trees, and the foliage of the understory trees and vines of the swamp forest join the green ballet. A mixture of alien sounds pervades the humid air. A reptile, slippery wet, emerges from a swamp pool, disturbing the other amphibians, who grunt and croak, much like farm animals at feeding time. A cicada-like din pulsates the air as in a midsummer woods. Cockroaches, spiders, and scorpions are numerous. Giant dragonflies, closer to our concept of swamp life, are the only flying creatures. [3]

The botanical life of this forest reveals weird branchings, angular and stiff, and strange differences in leaves and in the manner of growth. Yet there is pattern and order; we see plant communities in this odd landscape. And as with the insect and animal sounds, there are haunting similarities that bind these ancient plants to those we know today.

Dominant trees of this great Carboniferous forest are of the genus Lepidodendron. Better than a hundred feet high with trunk diameters of two to three feet, it compares to the oak of our modern forests in size and number of species.[4] Because of its key role in man's economic and social evolution, we shall call this genus "Coalmaker."

The Coalmakers have an orderly habit of branching. Most do not branch until nearly thirty feet from the base; indeed many grow a hundred feet or more in columns before the first branches. The branching is nearly always equal, in twos, and each subsequent division is also in twos. The dichotomous habit continues until its branches end in grasslike leaves or cones.[5]

Although Coalmaker foliage is uniformly slender, it varies in length from one species to another. The leaf of one variety is less than a half inch in length, while that of another variety is almost thirty inches long. The longest leaf seems to be no wider than an inch and a quarter. Apparently, Coalmaker

Coalmaker

The Carboniferous forest as portrayed in a diorama in the Insect Zoo at the Smithsonian Institution's Museum of Natural History. The Carboniferous era began 345 million years ago and lasted about 65 million years. In this age before man, the earth was dominated by giant *Lepidodendron* trees (the coalmakers), reptiles, and strange insects, one species of which looked like a dragonfly and had a two-and-a-half-foot wingspread.

leaves become progressively shorter as the trees grow older.[6]

As the breeze stirs through Coalmaker's slender branches and leaves, pendulous foot-long cones pour out smoky clouds of tiny spores and, like giant muffineers, generously powder the pools of water and wet hillocks below. Looking through the swamp thicket, we begin to sort out more and more Coalmaker species; in some places these towering lords claim exclusive domain, with only one species in an area.[7] Below the Coalmakers and other Carboniferous trees are smaller trees, most of them Horsetail Rushes, similar to the small scouring rush of today's temperate regions. These prehistoric rushes, which grow as high as fifty feet with one-foot-diameter trunks, are understory trees. They occupy an ecological niche similar to that served by modern blue beeches, redbuds, dogwoods, and shadbushes, all of which are dwarfed by oak, maple, and beech.[8] Closer to the swamp forest floor are more plants. Here Sphenophyllum, or "Wedge Leaf" when translated literally from the Greek, is the dominant genus. Sometimes upright, sometimes scrambling and climbing, its ecological role is like that of today's Japanese honeysuckle.[9]

But near the end of the Carboniferous age and at the beginning of the Permian, Coalmaker and associates are unable to survive an evolutionary swing. The lords of the swamp forest, benefactors of the industrial revolution, disappear, and giant tree ferns replace them in their arborescent niche. The largest of these is the genus Pecopteris, which with its many exotic species reminds us of a Victorian greenhouse. Pecopteris, from the Greek, means "Winglike Comb" or "Feather Comb"; one can imagine its patterns transformed into the fine grillwork and fencing of the late 1800s[10]. At the edge of the future Allegheny plateau, the Carboniferous and early Permian plants flourish and die to fulfill a seemingly appointed cyclic round.

A strong breeze stirs again, rippling the pools of shallow water, blowing up through the wedge leaves, turning and twisting through the rushes, and stirring the slender Coalmaker leaves. The foliage throbs in harmony with the rhythm of the sun. Each leaf unfolds for a whisper of time while its photocells wink to lock the sunlight in chemical bondage. Thus over millions of years Coalmaker forests are forged. Roots, trunks, bark, and leaves settle into a twenty-foot mass to become part of the swamp forest floor; increasing tons of pressure bear on the oxygenless matrix; great banks of peat evolve. Finally, a foot-thick layer of fossil fuel is created—coal. [11]

Coalmaker

2
First Man

The only object found with this burial [of an adolescent or child]. . .was the carpometacarpal or wing bone of a Snow Goose. . . . This bone was lying directly on top of the skull and would suggest that it was part of a feather headpiece, since its feathers would have made a striking headdress as they are pure white, tipped with black.

—Frank R. Corliss, Jr.,
"Folly Run Cairn No. 1, 18-Ga-54"[1]

In contrast to the millions of years that Coalmaker and associates reigned, the centuries during which prehistoric man lived in the North Branch Valley passed like the flickering of an eyelash. Based on artifacts found in similar Allegheny regions, archeologists believe that as early as 16,000 B.C., Paleo Indians, singly or in small bands, could well have hunted and gathered food plants in the misty highlands and small floodplains of the Upper Potomac. What is known for sure is that man was there by about 10,000 B.C. because projectile points* used by Early Archaic Indians have been found in the uplands swamps of Garrett County.[2]

Retreating glaciers, moderating climate, and changing ecology brought increased foraging and hunting in the uplands. Artifacts found indicate the definite presence of Late Archaic Indians in the Upper Valley from 3000 to 1000 B.C. Among the artifacts are arrow and spear points characterized by a confusing lack of uniformity

---

*Projectile point is a generic term that can apply to either an arrowhead or spearhead when the exact usage cannot be determined.

and a variety of styles, which archeologists tend to attribute to a scarcity of good stone. The rock formations of the Upper Valley may be rich in coal, but the stone is of poor quality for hunting points. It is assumed, therefore, that the Indians obtained a better grade of quartzite, rhyolite, and chert by collecting or trading in regions to the east or west. The scarcity of good local stone also accounts for the Indians' practice of recycling; they reworked broken points into smaller points and resharpened some points over and over again.[3]

For about two thousand years, from these late Archaic times until about one thousand years ago, no specific evidence exists of man in the Upper Valley. Indians in other regions, however, while continuing to hunt and gather wild food, were also beginning to practice some horticulture, growing squash and corn. Quite likely they found the narrow Upper Valley undesirable for such seminomadic settlements because of its small floodplain sites.[4]

During the Late Woodland or Late Prehistoric period (A.D. 1000 to 1600) a more substantial picture of early man emerges.* Excavations at three locations in the valley—a shelter cave near the ridge of the Great Backbone, a stockaded farm-village next to the Potomac, and a burial site on a crest high above the farm-village—have revealed in some detail how he lived, worked, and buried his dead.[5] New digs and research on artifacts found there continue to expand our understanding not only of the cultural links among these sites but of their relationship to the more advanced cultures of the Ohio-Mississippi valley and the eastern tribes of Pennsylvania and the Atlantic seaboard.

Sand Cave, the shelter cave, is on the side of a wooded ridge of the Great Backbone about fifteen miles northeast of the Fairfax Stone. It would have been an ideal temporary shelter for hunters and travelers, as well as a more permanent place of habitation. Framed by luxuriant

*Although the white men were present in some North American regions before 1600, archeologic sites in areas where he had not yet penetrated could be termed Late Prehistoric, particularly if the sites dated from the latter part of the period.

First Man

This archaeological dig at Cresaptown, Maryland, has uncovered another Monongahela village on the Potomac, eighteen miles northeast of the Folly Run site.

11

ferns, mosses, lichens, and wildflowers, the hundred-foot-long opening varies from two to six feet in height. The cave itself is formed of white to gray-brown stained sandstone. Large angular blocks of the sandstone, some up to eight feet long, form a jumble over much of the floor. The ceiling, an impressive irregular dome, rises from one to fifteen feet high. At the back of the cave, a hundred feet into the mountain, two small streams emerge, flow a short distance, and then disappear beneath the floor. A cold fog forms occasionally in the damp air.[6]

Along the entrance are dead embers and pieces of charcoal mixed with coarse sand and humus. The sand is black, blended with the embers from many fires. Here were two pits, a stone-lined one for fire, another for refuse. Arrow or spear points testify to many hunts and meals. Pottery brings to mind busy hands working with flake scrapers and bone awls around the smoky fire. A shell bead speaks not of utility but of more important qualities: protection, power, or beauty.

The artifacts of Sand Cave uncovered to date are all of the Late Woodland period, although the digs have yielded no evidence of cultivated plants associated with that culture. Archeologists believe that future digs may well uncover evidence of earlier occupation by the Paleo and Archaic people.[7]

The stockaded farm-village is about fourteen miles northeast of Sand Cave, where a small stream, Folly Run, flows easterly from the steep slope of the Great Backbone into the Potomac. In its isolation the Folly Run site, closest known prehistoric village to the Potomac's source, is much like the North Branch Valley itself.

The excavations here have been more extensive than those at Sand Cave. The artifacts belong to a particular culture of the Late Woodland or Late Prehistoric period termed Monongahela, a culture found in a considerable number of village sites to the northwest in the Monongahela Valley of the Ohio-Mississippi watershed.[8] In the manner of the Monongahela culture, the people of Folly Run probably built their dwellings along the inside of the stockade, leaving the village center open for religious or community activity. The stockade itself had no gate; the ends on one side overlapped, leaving enough space for a circuitous route into the village. The dwellings were of simple construction. The villagers embedded a circle of pilings in the ground, tied the tops together, and covered the dome-shaped framework with layers of bark. The digs have uncovered postmoulds indicating that the pilings used to build dwellings and stockades were of two sizes: three and one-half inches in diameter in one location, five inches in another.

The Folly Run people farmed on a ten-acre alluvial plain next to the village. Deer, elk, and wild turkey supplemented the Monongahela mainstay diet of corn, squash, and beans. Deep pits lined with river boulders were used for roasting or steaming food. Sherds of pottery collected from several locations within the village suggest that the culture could have changed during one continuous occupation over a number of decades. More likely, however, there were two discrete occupations, since the sherds in one location were tempered with limestone, the preferred material of the early Late Prehistoric period, while those found in the others were tempered with shell, which was used later in the period. To judge from the pottery sherds, this was a place of human habitation for some decades, a permanence that would not have been possible before the development of horticulture.[9]

The Folly Run villagers, just like the Sand Cave people, left a number of projectile points, as well as an unfinished fishing hook. Grinding slabs and stones again testify to the handicraft, and a fragment of a clay pipe and a sandstone puck show sophistication in leisure and social activity. Cut canine teeth, beads of bird bone, and what was evidently a pendant of cannel coal represent values and beliefs comparable to those imputed to the shell beads of Sand Cave.[10]

Cannel coal, which is shiny hard, is attractive for carvings and ornamentation. It is so different from most other objects in the primitive environment that special powers could have been ascribed to it. Lignite, or brown coal, was used for ornamentation by Hopis of the Southwest, and Northwest coast tribes used it as a paint ingredient.

Only the Hopis, however, are known to have burned coal for heating. They used it to fire pots and to warm living areas. What might have happened had the Monongahela culture developed coal as a fuel is a matter for almost irresistible speculation.[11]

As in other Monongahela-phase settlements, the archeologists uncovered burials in the village, among them the graves of four youngsters. Small slabs of stone covered two of them, obviously the remains of infants. By one was a small shell-tempered pottery container.[12]

On either side of Folly Run Village, isolating it and its farm tract, the forested slopes rise a precipitous thirty degrees to Allegheny ridges. Almost two miles to the west, on the crest of one of the thousand-foot ridges, is the third of the three Late Woodland or Late Prehistoric locations, a burial site marked by a number of stone mounds. The crest affords a great panoramic view of the mountains and valleys and, as if to mark it for special honor, the site is positioned to receive the first rays of the morning sun.

From the times of the earliest pioneers, treasure hunters and souvenir collectors have searched mounds or burial cairns such as these and others found along the Allegheny ridges overlooking the Monongahela, the Youghiogheny, and the Cheat, as well as the Upper Potomac. The first white men succumbed as quickly as men of today to the fascination of artifacts and their talisman-like ties to a mysterious, romantic past. Only one of the mounds above Folly Run Village was overlooked and escaped despoilment. It is one of the few, perhaps the last of its kind, to yield its contents for systematic study.[13]

This mound, at the apex of the ridge, was one of seven overlooking about ten smaller mounds to the east. It was of impressive size, ten feet across and four feet high. A foot-thick layer of smaller stones composed the top and covered larger flat sandstone slabs that sloped inward and upward at a forty-degree angle. Charcoal covered the original ground surface, and under each stone was a small pocket of charcoal.

Within the mound the early people had buried an adult

and a child. Both lay with their faces to the northeast. In the rib area of the adult was a projectile point of blue chert. Lying nearby were a smooth river pebble, a rough piece of crystal quartz, and a beautiful small triangular point of clear crystal.[14] Only one object was with the child—a carpometacarpal, or wing bone, of a Snow Goose. It lay on the child's skull and apparently was the remains of a striking feather headpiece of pure white feathers tipped with black. If so, this was the grave of no lowborn child but of a prince or princess.

Archeologists believe that the Folly Run villagers may well have been the people who for many decades made elaborate burials for their dead leaders and notables at the crests of these high ridges. Of particular significance is the fact that the artifacts from the North Branch Valley—a bead made of shell, a small pottery container in a child's grave, and part of a gorgeous headpiece in a carefully constructed burial mound—provide valuable information in themselves, suggesting interest in beauty and in life after death. As evidenced by the long isosceles triangle, the mounds or cairns seem to relate to the early period of the Monongahela culture. The Snow Goose headdress points to possible ties with prehistoric people of what is today eastern Pennsylvania. An artifact in a mound above the Youghiogheny dates it to as late as the time of the first white men.

Until the early 1980s Folly Run Village was apparently the only Monongahela-phase settlement found on the Atlantic seaboard side of the Great Backbone. The nearest known Monongahela-phase village site to the west of Folly Run is about twenty miles northwesterly, where Sang Run enters the Youghiogheny. Excavations have been made of a Monongahela village at Cresaptown, about eighteen miles to the northeast, and preliminary digs have been made of a Late Woodland site at Paw Paw, West Virginia, about thirty-five miles to the east. The culture, therefore, could have had more than several sites along the Potomac floodplains.[15]

There are significant gaps in our knowledge of trade, warfare, and social intercourse among the villagers of Folly Run, Sang Run, and similar Late Woodland or

Late Prehistoric villages of the region. Research to date raises questions about the migration of people, the flow of culture through forested mountains, and the evolution of agrarian technology—that is, the acquisition of tools and knowledge to grow enough food to sustain semi-permanent communities. We do know that horticultural technology gave communities some permanence and a favorable environment for the evolution of more complex social, political, and religious institutions. Similarly, we know that a network of trails made possible trade, cultural exchange, political activity, and warfare over large areas. One of the most important and extensive systems was a north-south chain of trails just east of the Alleghenies. With these trails the Iroquois operated a *pax Iroquoia*, using them to hold together subject tribes and to conduct warfare and trade over hundreds of miles, from the vicinity of the Great Lakes deep into Pennsylvania and beyond.

The northeast-southwest trend of the Allegheny mountains and valleys also provided natural thoroughfares. One of these, the North Branch Trail, followed the Potomac southwesterly to its source. There it became the Horseshoe Trail, which crossed the Great Backbone and joined the Seneca Trail, a more important route that ran from present-day Buffalo, New York, to what is now the state of Georgia. Another significant thoroughfare was the Great Warrior Path, which crossed the North Branch Valley about ten miles northeast of the Potomac's source. This was a principal east-west route over the Alleghenies between the Potomac's South Branch valleys and the Ohio River. Despite its connotation of warfare, however, the word "warrior"—common in the names of a number of Indian paths—did not refer to fighters alone, but to all able-bodied men, including hunters, traders, refugees, and ambassadors.[16]

Origins of the Great Warrior Path are as misty as the Allegheny ridges. Part of it was a buffalo trace or trail that the American bison* followed in traveling among licks, grazing grounds, and watering places. Although there were evidently no large herds of buffalo in what

*The American buffalo is, in correct zoological terms, of the genus *Bison*.

16

is present-day West Virginia and western Maryland, the animal lived throughout the region. Prime grazing areas were the glades of what is present-day Garrett County, Maryland. These were upland meadows of rich, waist-high grasses.

Whether the buffalo trace was the best route for the human traveler has been much discussed. Some point out that, since the animals avoided the laurel thickets and undergrowth along the streams and kept to the higher ground and ridges of the open forest, their trace was not necessarily direct but followed the gentlest grades and therefore was presumed the easiest route through any region. According to this line of reasoning, A.B. Hulbert maintains that the "buffalo, because of his sagacious selection of the most sure and most direct courses, has influenced the routes of trade and travel of the white race as much, possibly, as he influenced the course of the redmen in earlier days."[17] Others considered the buffalo to have been a poor trailmaker. George Washington, who devoted great effort to planning and designing a transportation route across the Alleghenies, commented that a buffalo trace was nothing more "than their tracks from one lick to another and consequently was crooked and not well-chosen."[18] Reviewing the evidence, one concludes that although the buffalo trace and the Great Warrior Path may have coincided occasionally in crossing the North Branch Valley, the quality of the buffalo paths was such that neither prehistoric men nor early white men slavishly followed them in their travels.

Nevertheless, a body of tales, folklore, and tradition—even though vague, apocryphal, and sometimes contradictory—supports the idea that trails like the Great Warrior Path embodied ties to wise forces from the past, and that they were in a stream of native intelligence that began with the migratory beast and progressed through the noble savage to the romantic pioneer. It was thus perhaps only natural that the nineteenth-century followers of this tradition—the highway and railroad builders who opened up the wilderness—carried with them an aura of right purpose.

3

Unlocking the North Branch Valley

*...& one object of my journey being to obtain
information of the nearest and best communication between the Eastern & Western Waters;
& to facilitate...the Inland Navigation of the
Potomack....*

—Washington's Diary of September 1784[1]

As white men came to the North Branch Potomac
region, they used the Indian paths. Some followed the
ancient tribal highways along the southwesterly pattern
of the Allegheny ranges. Others rode and tramped the
Great Warrior Path, which, by the 1770s, had come to
be known as McCullogh's Pack Horse Path.

McCullough, a major in the French and Indian War,
is described in disparate legends as both a villain who
sold firearms to the Indians and a hero who led a relief
expedition to Fort Henry on the Ohio. His path was far
from direct, for some sections surely followed a buffalo
trace, but it offered easy grades for those who traveled
eastward toward the seaboard or westward toward the
Ohio-Mississippi basin. Between the Potomac and the
Great Backbone it crossed a mountain meadow where,
sometime before the Revolution, a settler identified in
the records only by his last name, Ryan, built a cabin.
For years thereafter, Ryan's Glade was a stopping place
where horses and cattle could browse on rich waist-high
forage and travelers could replenish larders with game.

Another pioneer mentioned in the records of the period is the Reverend John Taylor, an itinerant Baptist minister who followed McCullough's Path between the North Branch Potomac and the Cheat rivers between 1772 and 1781, preaching in isolated settlements on and off the way. From accounts of the period, he met the adversities of the frontier with a fiery determination to make the glades ring with the glory of God.[2]

Among the early settlers were Mennonites and German-Swiss Amish from Pennsylvania, who followed the southwesterly drift of the mountain terrain. They built handsome farms in the fertile lands of Garrett County, where they found the isolation of the wilderness edge congenial to their religious aspirations.

Of some of the early pioneers, comparatively little is known. For several different reasons, one of them being that the fight for survival left little time for log keeping, they left few historical records. Dunkers (Tunkers), another Anabaptist group of early settlers who, like the Amish, refused to take oaths or bear arms, even disallowed statistics of church membership because they would encourage "undesirable pride."[3] British deserters from the Revolution and conscientious objectors who fled to these western regions also welcomed the anonymity of the frontier; understandably, they had little interest in keeping exact records and dates.[4]

The westernmost streams, those that extended the Potomac watershed into the edge of the Alleghenies, stirred particularly keen interest almost from the moment of discovery. One reason was that, in his Charter of 1632, King Charles I designated "Potowmack's first fountain" as the beginning point of Maryland's southern and western border. Also keyed to this spring were the lands deeded to Lord Fairfax and those belonging to the colony of Virginia. There were, however, several westerly branches of the Potomac that began on the Alleghenies' rugged edge, and the question was, which of these sprang from the "first fountain." Contingent on the answer was the valid ownership of land in a growing number of settlements in western Maryland and western Virginia, and to find the answer became a matter of increasing urgency. So, under the leadership of Colonel William Mayo, commissioners set out in 1736 and traced the North Branch Potomac through vast forests to a spring near the ridge that divided the two great watersheds. This was determined to be "the first fountain." Ten years later, a second party of commissioners placed the Fairfax Stone at this same spring.* The stone prevailed against more than a century of challenges as the legal marker of the 1632 Charter of King Charles.[6]

After the Revolution came more surveyors under the leadership of Francis Deakins of Georgetown. West of Fort Cumberland and near the Fairfax Stone, they laid out more than four thousand fifty-acre lots for Maryland veterans.[7]

Meanwhile, commercial and political leaders searched tirelessly for ways to move people and goods more quickly and efficiently to the transmontane. George Washington was one of the most diligent. Since 1759 he had advocated a water-highway route through Virginia's Alleghenies. Once free of wartime duties, he renewed his efforts and in September 1784 led a month-long, six-hundred-mile expedition by horseback up the Potomac, over the Alleghenies to the Ohio River. His small party included three servants; his 25-year-old nephew, Bushrod Washington; Dr. James Crank, his family physician of long standing, and Dr. Crank's son.[8]

Washington's journey also gave him an opportunity to reinforce his legal rights to western land holdings, which his years of Revolutionary campaigns had not permitted him to do. In certain instances his extensive land holdings, some as far away as the Ohio basin, were being subjected to the ambiguities and challenges of frontier law. At that time, possession—a cabin and a cornfield—backed up by a musket was adequate to establish ownership.[9]

Although Washington undoubtedly had in mind the

---

*The Journal of Thomas Lewis, a member of the second group of commissioners, tells of the great forest that stood at the Potomac's source: "Exceedingly well timbred with such as very Large Spruce Pines, great multitudes of Beach and Shugartrees, Cherry trees—the most and finest I ever saw—some 3 or 4 feet in diameter, 30 or 40 feet without a branch," and "some few oaks, chestnuts and Locusts."[5]

potential effect of a commercial route west on his personal holdings, the national interest motivated him even more. In particular, he found that delay in developing such a route could mean the loss to European holdings in Canada and Louisiana of both political allegiances and the trade of western settlers. At the same time, he was well aware that leaders in Pennsylvania, Maryland, and New York were also keen in their pursuit of a trade route west. As a Virginian, he had a parochial inclination to find a route that would be entirely within the boundaries of Virginia.[10] He had personally inspected the area north of the Allegheny range, which provided easy access to Lake Erie and the west.

As the general and his party pushed through the forests and sparsely settled country, he found ample opportunity to gather advice and information from settlers, agents, and friends who gathered to meet with him when informed of his coming. Early in the journey he met with General Dan Morgan, frontier hero of the Revolution, who advised him that a road was being considered from Winchester to the west, which, though going through Maryland, would not cross into Pennsylvania. Washington obtained estimates of distances and descriptions of the mountain terrain and river conditions. As best he could, he corroborated whatever he was told. But intelligence was often secondhand, even vague, and there was good reason to question the objectivity of those informants whose own holdings might be affected by a proposed land route.[11]

Torrents, rapids, and rocky ledges abound in the Alleghenies. The engineering needed in Washington's day to make a stream navigable to a point high in its watershed and close to the dividing ridge was matched only by the boulders and cliffs obstructing a portage route over the ridge line to an equally navigable stream in the next watershed. Although Washington's chronicle is practically devoid of comment as to hardship, memory of frontier campaigns, or wilderness beauty, the journey was arduous. The food was poor. His party usually slept without shelter, and they were often exposed to soaking autumn rains.[12]

After inspecting his land claims to the southwest of present-day Pittsburgh, Washington began his return to Mount Vernon. Heading southeast and following McCullough's Path, he entered Maryland and crossed the Youghiogheny, the last stream in the Ohio-Mississippi watershed. He followed the path over Backbone Mountain into the North Branch Valley at Ryan's Glade and forded the Potomac about ten miles from the Fairfax Stone. His journey continued up the eastern side of the valley, across Stony Creek, and over the Allegheny Front. Traveling homeward, he continued to question all he met, asking again and again about the best way west.[13]

Washington's exploration was a great success. With the chronicle of his trip and the authority of an admired leader of the Revolution, he set forth a persuasive course of action. On his recommendation, the Virginia and Maryland legislatures moved quickly to authorize the Patowmack Company. By late summer of 1785, with Washington as president, the company started to build a navigable passage intended initially to run between Washington and Cumberland. The plan combined several devices: canals around the five most formidable Potomac barriers, including the rapids at Harpers Ferry and Great Falls; low-level dams to divert water into deepened channels or sluices; the widening and deepening of the river in some areas, and the removal of boulders in others. Connection to the Ohio was to be made by overland portage from the Potomac's highest navigable point.[14]

Until the early 1820s the Patowmack Company improved navigation and collected tolls between Cumberland and Washington. Eventually, however, the river's annual extremes—wild spring freshets and low water in late summer and fall—forced the company fiscally and literally aground. Thereupon, dreams of merchants and investors, through the use of the old company's stock, evolved into a new enterprise, the Chesapeake and Ohio Canal Company. Pledged to thwart the river's erratic flow, the new company planned a continuous 184-mile canal between Washington and Cumberland. Although the exact connection between the Potomac watershed and the Ohio-Mississippi was still undetermined, the Board of Army Engineers proposed to Congress in the early 1820s a North Branch route almost identical to the one strongly favored by Washington.[15]

Enthusiasm for canals was running high, and for good reasons. The Erie, completed in 1825, had quickly demonstrated speed and economy in the transport of goods. Therefore, on the Fourth of July 1828, just north of Georgetown in the District of Columbia, President John Quincy Adams broke ground for the Chesapeake and Ohio Canal. A military band played, soldiers fired salutes, and Adams's classical oratory favorably compared the new endeavor to the pyramids of Egypt.

On the same day in Baltimore, Charles Carroll of Carrollton, the revered, ninety-year-old Maryland statesman, broke ground for the Baltimore and Ohio Railroad. Watching from a perch on his father's shoulders was a five-year-old boy, Henry Gassaway Davis, and at that moment the Sibyl of steam must have made a prophecy: this youngster will start as a brakeman on the B & O, and he'll vault to wealth with his own railroad developing the Allegheny's coal and timber.[16]

Railroading, however, was in its noisy childhood, and water-portage routes had hardly been an unqualified success, so the highways still remained the proven way of transport. Indeed, the federal government had funded and, in 1819, completed its first interstate—the Great National Pike from Cumberland to Wheeling. With such considerations in mind, the Virginia legislature incorporated the Northwestern Road Company in February 1827 for the building of a highway on a long proposed route west from Winchester through Romney to Parkersburg on the Ohio. The road was planned to avoid Pennsylvania territory and go through larger towns with a potential source of stock subscribers. The idea had fiscal merit but necessitated a route through harsh mountainous terrain that soon stalled construction; the sale of stock declined and the future of the road company seemed bleak.

So in 1831 the legislature reincorporated the company,

renaming it the Northwestern Turnpike Road Company, and the Virginia treasury provided financing with reimbursement from tolls collected every twenty miles. The highway could now follow easier grades across the glades and mountains. Virginia's chief engineer for highways, General Claudius Crozet, former officer of artillery for Napoleon, completed the new route in 1837. Benjamin Latrobe termed it "the finest mountain road in the country."[17] When the turnpike reached the North Branch Valley, it closely followed Washington's proposed portage route—McCullough's Pack Horse Path—across the Potomac, and the crossing was named North Branch.

Life at the edge of the wilderness was usually one of big families and active enterprise. Jacob Schaeffer, a descendant of German immigrants from Lebanon, Pennsylvania, settled in North Branch toward the end of the 1830s. Altogether the Schaeffers had thirteen children. His thirteen-year-old son, James Henry, helped him build the first house—a log building—which also served for storage. With a wealth of timber at hand, the family became involved in a growing tanning enterprise and cabinet trade, constructing bedsteads, bureaus, and sofas. Schaeffer operated a tollgate and maintained an inn for turnpike travelers; at the turn of the decade he became known as the first postmaster, at which time the settlement was renamed Schaeffersville.

Settlers' wagons rolled west. Drovers herded turkeys, geese, hogs, sheep, and cattle; four- and six-horse teams hauled loads of flour, pork, salt, iron, coal, and furniture. By 1845, three fast stages a week operated between Winchester and Parkersburg. Hog and cattle drivers sometimes damaged the turnpike when they traveled it too early in the spring, but new macadam kept it in fairly good condition until the Civil War.[18]

At midcentury, commerce and the travelers' vitality grew as if fueled by energy fresh from the land. America's leaders and poets glorified man's taming of the wilderness. On the western horizon was the vision of a republic, its agrarian and democratic virtues elevated to new heights by man's industry and great new machines. One writer, reflecting the mood of the times, asserted that it was not too extreme to say that George Washington had awakened the wilderness, the slothful giant of the west, from a millenium of sleep to "a wonderful life that is the marvel of the centuries."[19]

Romantic expression suited the day. Philip Pendleton Kennedy of Martinsburg, who wrote as the "Clerke of Oxenforde," conveyed popular faith in America's development in especially vivid prose.[20] In June 1851 Kennedy and four companions, all Virginia gentlemen, traveled the Northwestern Turnpike to the Potomac headwaters for fishing and exploration of the valleys surrounding the Fairfax Stone. Crossing the Potomac at Schaeffersville, the gentlemen rode up "a long fair sweep" to an inn called Winston "on the brow of a lofty hill overlooking the Potomac."[21]

> The castle of Winston stands, like the castle of Richmond, "fair on the hill"; and although it did not greet our eyes with the feudal grandeur of Norham—with warders on the turrets, donjon keep, loop hole grates where captives weep, and the banner of St. George flapping idly in the breeze, as that famous hold met the gaze of Marmion...it looked cheerful and pleasant enough....[22]

As they prepared for their forays, the proprietor of Winston assured the party that the trout were available in great abundance; he himself had recently caught two to three hundred before breakfast. Kennedy's party itself then proceeded to catch more than two hundred on their first day and even more on the second, overindulging themselves with what they perceived as nature's infinite bounty.

Kennedy repeatedly describes these fishing ventures in military terms, likening them to one of Caesar's expeditions with "many points of resemblance to those so famous of the splendid Roman," and describing his party as waging "unceasing war throughout this Potomac region." Finally, "having invaded some of the large tributary streams," they ended their campaign in victory: "the wild tribes that invaded the Alleghenies fled before our arms." Prophetically, Kennedy sees the trout as the "enemy," symbol of all the wilderness creatures later to be set upon with abandon.[23]

At the end of these fatiguing but merry adventures, the Virginians speculate on the future of the virgin forests and wildlife. Two contrasting visions emerge: one of prosperous plantations and an idyllic country life, the other of a productive place of commerce. In the first vision, two of the party, Peter and Adolphus, see themselves as great cattle farmers, each with fifty thousand acres on the slopes of the Backbone. During the summer their mansions would be filled

> with gentlemen and ladies, who hunted and rode, fished, eat [sic] the trout, the broils, and roasts and pastries of the deer with bear's meat, and panther or wild-cat collops—grew fat and defied the world below in the pastimes of the wilderness—then a wilderness made easy of ingress and egress by fine graded roads, cut out by the great proprietors, Peter and Galen—whose two castles of old Saxon architecture, built on either slope of the mountain would enable the Backbone to frown down on the Potomac on the one side, on the Blackwater the other.[24]

These romantics also call for a tower with "lounges and cushions of the softest—with a harp or so, and two or three grand pianos, to play swelling themes in accord with the sublime music of the torrent roaring down the Alleganies!"[25]

Kennedy, however, visualizes a second future. He points out that development must be more than great parks, baronial castles with huge fireplaces, and gentlemen and ladies chasing game through the forests. It should be a proper businesslike venture:

> The railroad must put this noble country alongside the sea; and the forest must be cleared away for the plough, and the waterpower everywhere must be used, and the coal dug out of the earth, and the ores, the gypsum, the salt, and the lumber, turned into wealth; and therefore the land (such land! that can be bought now from sixty cents to a dollar an acre!) must be worth fifty dollars—and that at no very distant day.[26]

Kennedy seems to have the fervor and inspiration of a present-day Isaiah: man's technology will tame the wilderness!

Unlocking the Valley

> All this is to be done by the hardy enterprise of men in whose souls poetry and imagination are not predominant—by men with necessity at their elbow, who are resolute upon acquisition, and who have been trained to the rougher realities of life; not by a set of daintily-nurtured gentlemen, to whom life has been but little else than an agreeable pastime.[27]

One who would grow to mastery of this "hardy enterprise" was Henry Gassaway Davis.

4

Making the Way Straight

Disce ut semper victurus; vive ut eras
moriturus.

*Work as if you were to live forever; live as if
you were to die to-morrow.*

> —Charles M. Pepper
> Frontispiece, *The Life and Times
> of Henry Gassaway Davis*[1]

Caleb Davis was an enterprising young merchant
when, on July 4, 1828, he took his family to the laying
of the cornerstone for the Baltimore and Ohio Railroad.
This development not only represented Baltimore's best
hope for beating other seaboard cities to the western
market but promised more and greater opportunities for
the city's commercial community. Intoxicated by the
prospects, Caleb rapidly expanded his business interests,
building houses and developing small factories in the
Patapsco River corridor of the growing rail line. Like
other Baltimore entrepreneurs, he also contracted to do
grading for the B & O.

Henry Davis was a youngster during these busy years
and spent much of his time with friends of well-to-do
families on the large farms of central Maryland. While
he developed a fondness for agriculture and rural life,
he sensed that his father, by leveling a route for the
railroad, was opening the way to an excitingly different
future.

For the Davis family, however, that future did not

come as hoped for. Caleb had pledged his own resources on the bonds of fellow contractors and had generally over-extended his business ventures. With the economic panic of 1837, the family was reduced to poverty. When Caleb proved unable to deal with the ensuing emotional crisis, his wife, Louisa Warfield, took over responsibility for the family's support. Fourteen-year-old Henry, one of six children, left school to become a breadwinner.

For a while, Henry worked as a waterboy and did odd jobs. Then, aware of the family's severe circumstances, former Governor George Howard offered him a job at Waverley, his plantation in the central Maryland farm region near Baltimore.* Here young Davis took on suc-cessively responsible tasks and soon reached a position of trust, keeping plantation accounts and distributing stores to the slaves.[2]

When he turned twenty, Henry became a brakeman on the B & O. He had a physique inured to heavy farm work. He also had a growing business sensibility. These, combined with a strong entrepreneurial drive and a religiously inspired work ethic, gave him all the qualities essential for success in the evolving industrial age.

As he was to do all his life, Henry drew strength and confidence from the Presbyterian-Calvinist beliefs of the Davis home. He even found a profitable lesson in his father's rise and fall. Caleb Davis, by diligence and hard work, had provided his family with ample goods of the world, and for him to be rewarded for such diligence was consistent with Protestant teaching. However, Caleb had made an error in judgment, placing his trust in others and pledging his own resources in support of their loans; in the ensuing panic they dragged him to ruin. This was a key lesson for Henry: one should rely on one's own talents and be in a position to control one's own destiny.

From his mother's example he drew another lesson. Louisa Warfield had supported the family with years of hard work running a girl's school. She taught him to see poverty as no disgrace but rather as a part of God's

*George Howard was son of the Revolutionary War hero, John Eager Howard, who built Waverley.

Henry Gassaway Davis in his prime, with his mother, Louisa Warfield.

plan; one should work to overcome adversity and should be neither ashamed of it nor resigned to it. In later years young men who joined the Davis enterprises found that advancement came not only through fidelity but also through a demonstrated capacity for work, a willingness to save money, and a commitment to the principle of self-help.[3]

A brakeman's job in the primitive railroading of the 1840s was dangerous and demanding, and there were ample opportunities to demonstrate leadership. Once, young Davis took over at a train accident when passengers and workers looked to him for direction. On another occasion he persuaded company officials to let him manage the company's first night operation, which he carried out with gratifying success.[4] Adapting well to the railroad management system, he became a conductor and, by 1847, manager of the line between Baltimore and Cumberland.

The B & O rails extended farther and farther from Baltimore—south to Washington, west to Frederick, and beyond to the Alleghenies. By 1851 they had reached Piedmont, a handful of houses at the foot of the Great Backbone, barely fifty miles northeast of the Fairfax Stone. From here the B & O climbed the Backbone and crossed the Alleghenies into the Ohio-Mississippi watershed. In 1853 it arrived in Wheeling.

The long steep grade to the west made Piedmont a key B & O terminal. Observing the area with his eye for profit, Henry saw a rich potential. At his request, in 1854, he was made station agent for Piedmont. During his first year there, he lived in a boxcar while building a home for his Frederick County bride, Katherine Ann Bantz.

Henry Davis's entrepreneurial nature soon thrust him into the other half of nineteenth-century railroading: resource development. First, he established his brother in a Piedmont coal and lumber business. Then, in 1858, he shed the protective and instructive coat of the B & O, resigned as station agent, took over the management of the coal and lumber business, and founded the Piedmont Savings Bank with himself as president.[5]

The Civil War accelerated railroad technology and at the same time became a ravenous consumer. Not surprisingly, the war spurred Henry Davis on to more intense activity. He began supplying the Union army with horses, coal for military locomotives, and thousands of railroad ties and bridge timbers to replace those burned by Confederate marauders.[6]

The wartime supply mission sharpened Davis's ability to locate raw materials and deliver needed products. By the war's end he owned thousands of acres of timberland on both sides of the Great Backbone. Typical of these holdings was an outstanding headwaters pine forest within the tract that Francis Deakins had surveyed for veterans of the Revolution. For this magnificent virgin forest, underlaid with coal, Davis paid fifty cents an acre for one thousand acres.

About this same time he added a political dimension to his career by winning a seat in the West Virginia House of Delegates in 1866, and his legislative work began to bear fruit as abundantly as his commercial endeavors. From his first session of statutory labor he returned with a charter for the Potomac and Piedmont Railroad Company. He also returned with charters for two new counties, Mineral and Grant; carved from larger, farmer-dominated counties to form the southeast side of the North Branch from Piedmont to the Fairfax Stone, these new counties were more politically agreeable to the construction of a railroad southwesterly along the river valley.[7] Although Davis was no longer with the B & O, its executives still thought of him as their protégé, and they encouraged him to build a feeder line there, knowing that it would provide traffic and revenues for their trunk line.[8]

Political considerations were integral to railroad ventures, just as they were to canal and turnpike endeavors, and Henry Davis continued to prosper both as a businessman and a politician. His wealth grew with the harvest of magnificent virgin timber in Garrett County, west of the North Branch Valley over the Backbone, an enterprise that centered in the new town of Deer Park, where he had an impressive farm. There, his logging and lumbering projects were extensive. Timber came from various forests in Garrett County to the Davis lumberyard and was shipped to points east and west on the B & O. He also operated a sizable sheep and cattle acreage, exhibiting a commitment to agriculture that was more than just political rhetoric. Farming can bring wholesome satisfactions, unlike any to be derived from the more exploitative aspects of logging and lumbering, and his journals reflect a sincere fondness for it.[9] His political fortunes had so prospered that by 1871 he was United States senator from West Virginia.[10]

Deer Park, where Senator Davis spent most of the year when he wasn't in Washington, was an attractive holiday spot for notables and prominent government leaders of the late 1800s. High on the cool, pleasant Allegheny plateau and an easy five-hour train ride from the steamy dog days of Washington's July and August, this town, primarily a B & O resort village, developed a certain prestigious political ambience. In 1883 Hallie and Stephen Elkins* had General and Mrs. Ulysses Grant as their guests. In '89 the Davises entertained President Benjamin Harrison, Secretary of the Treasury William Windom and his wife, and Attorney General William Miller. Other prominent Deer Park visitors during these decades were Cardinal Gibbons of Baltimore, William Jennings Bryan, William McKinley (before he became president), and philanthropist-banker W.W. Corcoran.[11]

But the guests who created the most excitement were President Cleveland and his bride, Frances Folsom. At the president's request, Senator Davis arranged their 1886 honeymoon in one of the B & O's "Mountain Chalet Cottages." It was an occasion characterized by informal social events and outings. Cleveland liked to fish and enjoyed excursions along the Garrett County streams and ponds. Unbeknownst to the president, one of the Davis sons would put an ample quantity of trout in Cleveland's basket to make sure he would have the satisfaction of a good catch.[12]

Davis's philosophy as a conservative Democrat evolved from a blend of home-derived work ethic, agrarian experience in a plantation setting, and economic requirements of development. Davis empathized with the South and its culture, opposing test oaths and Negro suffrage.** He enunciated the Jeffersonian virtues of an agrarian way of life: nations that neglect their agriculture decay; those that encourage it survive. After all, 75 percent of the signers of the Declaration of Independence were agriculturalists and four American presidents had been farmers.[13] Nevertheless, despite this faith in the strength of rural culture, Davis had been convinced at the beginning of the war that the North's industrial might

*Stephen Elkins, the delegate from New Mexico, had married Hallie, Davis's daughter, in 1875.

**Test oath laws passed by Congress and some state legislatures following the Civil War prescribed oaths of past allegiance to the Union for such groups as teachers, preachers, attorneys, jurors, voters, and government officials.

would bring a sure victory; thus, he had opposed Virginia's secession and supported the Union.

After the war, he proposed development policies—low taxes, economical administration of state affairs, a "hearty welcome" to capitalists and laborers, and "liberal encouragement" to immigrants to make West Virginia their home—to utilize the new state's rich resources.[14] He knew firsthand that coal was a "manufactured" article, requiring skill and labor in production, and that it needed protection; therefore, he supported a tariff on imported coal, which would provide the "incidental protection" popular among conservative Democrats and help West Virginia, a poor economic relative to northern and western states.[15] Refusing the nomination for governor of West Virginia in 1888, he said, "I think the people ought to nominate...[the] man ...[who] would be of most service in developing...[the] great resources of the state."[16]

Henry Davis had found support for this ideology among his Senate colleagues when, beginning in 1880, he at last started at Piedmont to build the Potomac and

Finance committee of the West Virginia Central Railway. Henry Davis is standing at center. The bearded official at right is James G. Blaine, "the plumed knight of Maine," secretary of state under presidents Garfield and Arthur and Republican candidate for president in 1884.

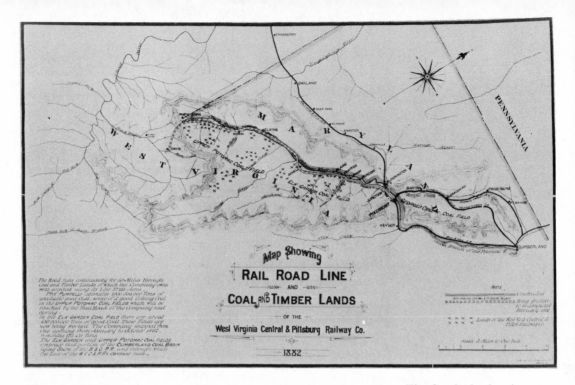

Map Showing
RAIL ROAD LINE
AND
COAL AND TIMBER LANDS
OF THE
West Virginia Central & Pittsburg Railway Co.
1882

Piedmont Railroad up the misty, rich North Branch Valley toward the Fairfax Stone and the great coal fields and forests of the Blackwater beyond. A year later the less prestigious name, Potomac and Piedmont, was replaced with West Virginia Central and Pittsburg. The new charter also expanded the company's grants of power: West Virginia Central could buy and sell real estate; build furnaces; mine coal, iron ore, and other minerals; and buy, sell, and manufacture lumber. Although the company could not engage in banking, it could build to connect with the Chesapeake and Ohio "or any other railroad company."[17] The senator-railroad builder made full use of the potentials of his railroad's charter.

By the fall of 1881, Davis's crews had laid twelve and a half miles of rail. Tramways and inclined planes connected the railroad to Elk Garden, West Virginia, and from there the company began to ship the high quality, semibituminous coal from the Big Vein mine on October 20. Formal opening of the railroad's first section was on November 2, a fine fall day. Senator Davis and a party of notables came by his own West Virginia Central from Piedmont. In addition to his Senate colleague Thomas Bayard of Delaware and his son-in-law, Stephen Elkins, there were Major Alexander Shaw, capitalist John

The Cumberland and Potomac coal basin and the line of the West Virginia Central Railway.

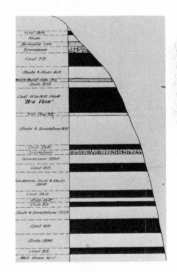

Geological section of the Elk Garden coal field.

35

Hambleton, and Governor William Hamilton of Maryland. It was, Davis told the assembled throng, "a momentous event for the whole region."

The next day, accompanied by reporters from the *Baltimore Sun* and the *Baltimore American*, Davis led several members of his party to the Potomac headwaters and Blackwater region. Once again coal and timber resources were reported beyond expectation.[18]

West Virginia Central made a second opening on the Big Vein at Elk Garden in 1883. The company now had three hundred men in its mining department. By August passenger and freight trains made regular thirty-two-mile runs up the valley to Elkins. Formerly Schaeffersville, the town had been renamed in honor of Stephen Elkins. An associate of the senator in his West Virginia development efforts, Elkins later served as a Republican senator from West Virginia.[19]

Five mines, three owned by West Virginia Central, and sixteen sawmills were at work along the line in 1885. The road pushed up the valley, past the Fairfax Stone, and into the Blackwater Valley and the Ohio-Mississippi watershed, a perfect catalyst for the timbering and mining, which now began to accelerate exponentially. Conversion, reduction, and removal of wood and coal took place at lightning speeds, in striking contrast to the glacial rate at which they had been formed. The summer schedule was two trains daily: one a regular passenger and mail train, the other a mixed train—passenger and freight. During the winter only the mixed train was maintained. Service had now reached Davis, West Virginia, almost sixty miles from Piedmont. Here a tannery was in operation and the company opened a hotel.[20]

By 1889, Leadville, West Virginia, eighty-five miles from Piedmont, became West Virginia Central's headquarters and rail center. Henry Davis and Stephen Elkins built new homes here, Queen Anne-style mansions of lavish proportions. Leadville, destined to be a significant commercial center, was also renamed Elkins, and Elkins, on the Northwestern Turnpike, now became Gorman, in honor of Maryland senator Arthur Pue Gorman, president of the C & O Canal in 1872 and a heavy

Judge Parker, left, and Henry Davis.

"GET OFF THE TRACK!"

investor in West Virginia Central's stocks.[21] The adjoining village across the Potomac in West Virginia was named Gormania.

Thus, mill towns, mining towns, and West Virginia Central stations from Piedmont to the Fairfax Stone became a constellation of names memorializing leaders of what came to be called the Industrial Age. The West Virginia Central was known popularly as the Senatorial Railroad since six towns bore the names of Senate colleagues who purchased stock. In addition to Gorman and Bayard, there were William Windom of Minnesota, later secretary of the treasury under Garfield; Jerome Chaffee of Colorado; Johnson Camden of West Virginia; and James G. Blaine, the "plumed knight" of Maine and a Republican friend of business and industry. Blaine also served on West Virginia Central's board of directors as

In 1904 the Democratic Party, having lost the presidency twice with populist William Jennings Bryan, turned to a more conservative candidate, Judge Alton B. Parker, of New York. Henry Davis was named to run with him as vice president, but even though the two were portrayed as safe and reliable defenders of the gold standard they were no match for the colorful incumbent, Theodore Roosevelt. The popular reaction, which gave Roosevelt a plurality of more than two million votes, was anticipated by this pre-election cartoon in *Judge*.

Henry Gassaway Davis. The official campaign portrait, 1904.

did Arthur Gorman. Places were also named for William Barnum, president of the Hoosatanic Railroad and senator from Connecticut; August Schell, Tammany Society sachem who placed part of the railroad's bonds; and Benjamin Harrison, senator from Indiana at the close of Davis's term and twenty-third president of the United States.[22]

Congressional peers could see a certain solidness in Henry Gassaway Davis, the businessman and senator. His diligence, hard work, and attention to detail distinguished him sharply from some of the rail barons of the Gilded Age. His railroad represented more than just a sound investment; it represented a sound ideal. Although he wasn't president of a great trunk line through important northern cities, his work in the Senate and on the edge of the West Virginia wilderness demonstrated the virtues that businessmen and politicians have always extolled as the fiber of American democracy. Though there were surely some patronizing smiles, his envious colleagues sensed that Henry Davis was working close to the American mother lode.

Davis prospered from the bountiful timber and coal, the God-given fruits of the earth, through perseverance, self-help, and hard work. He made his way in the world as he found it, working within the constraints of development techniques, and there is no evidence of deceit in his character. Others had the same opportunity to benefit from nature's largess. He encouraged them to follow his example.

To one who can sense the former beauty of this valley and mountainous region of once primeval forest, only greed or an alien ethic can explain its exploitation by nineteenth-century developers. Nor is it any easier to understand their abuse of human resources. To Davis and most of the other developers, however, the hard and sometimes cruel life of the workers—the miners, the railway laborers, the lumbermen—was the natural fulfillment of Social Darwinism, which they saw as a necessity in the evolution of labor and technology and as a prerequisite for progress.[23]

It is doubtful that Henry Davis understood the interactions or sensed the consequences of his wilderness harvest. But it is also doubtful whether man's margin of wisdom today has yet grown enough to offset the consequences of his increasingly sophisticated technology and exploitative skills. Ironically, with our present knowledge, we probably have less confidence in the future than did Henry Davis as he set forth in his march into the virgin forests in the days of the West Virginia Central.

* * * * * * *

The grandeur of the virgin forests and the abundance of wildlife at the wilderness edge were recurring sources of wonder during these decades. West Virginia Central reported to its stockholders in the 1880s:

> The coal and iron ore lands are covered with a primeval forest of black walnut, cherry, white spruce, ash, hemlock, maple and poplar.[24]

> The coal area is a thick forest almost covered with spruce and hemlock, the trees being of enormous size and good quality, making it as superior in its timber as it is in coal.[25]

The sounds and images of the first logging of this primeval forest must have had the charm of a Currier and Ives print: a husky lumberman doing battle with a three-hundred-year-old Canadian hemlock; the alternate burring and rasping of the saw; sawdust flakes forming golden pyramids around a reddish-brown trunk; the squealing of tortured wood at the beginning of a majestic fall; and finally a thunderous crash. Then, as in another Currier and Ives print, a logging train clatters through snow-laden wood and spouts cumulus white steam against a clear blue sky; the train passes, and the only sound in the valley is the wind in the pines, like a human sigh.[26]

Technology asserting itself in the forest reached a zenith in the Shay, a logging locomotive especially designed for the Upper Potomac and other timber areas. Every wheel of the Shay had its own drive shaft, enabling it to negotiate rough, uneven track, light rails, and steep grades. One commentator wrote, "with pistons and cranks frantically threshing...from...front...to rear..., everything about the machine seemed alive."[27]

But these romanticized scenes of wilderness invasion were a melancholy counterpoint to the dismal aftermath of clearcut lumbering. Timber harvest along the Upper Potomac was total—cut as close as possible to include everything marketable. Like the upright bayonets of fallen soldiers, the jagged wood was silhouetted stark against the sky. Uncontrolled fires swept these remains of "slashings," and new growth was delayed for years. Where the land was not made into farms, the rain gathered in torrents and, unimpeded, tore off top soil and the little remaining humus. Sawdust from the mills became a problem; Buffalo and Abram creeks were heavily laden with mill and mine waste. In dry weather particularly, the river had a "foul appearance," as mats of sawdust built up in solid bars along the water's edge.[28]

Canadian hemlock, prevalent in some places along the river valley and the West Virginia Central line, was valuable for tanning. In contrast to the earlier cottage-scale works, the railroad generated factory-sized tanneries. There were substantial plants at Parsons and Bayard, and in 1890, Hoffman and Co. of Wheeling built a large tannery at Gorman that employed up to 150 men and could process three hundred hides a day. Thus, more and more tan liquor and lime water poured into the river, and the floods washed tan bark from the banks.[29]

Across the small Potomac in Gormania, D.J. Bosley operated a sawmill that produced hemlock and oak lumber, cross ties, and wood pulp.[30] Another share of pollution was added to the burdened waters when a "number of Eastern gentlemen" erected a large pulp and paper plant at West Piedmont. The mill needed quantities of white spruce, which West Virginia Central boasted was "in great abundance on its line."[31]

Some of the processed timber never left the valley since coal mines were heavy users of wood. Cross ties were needed for the mining railroad, and the rails themselves were made from twelve-foot-long two-by-four timbers. "Sets" of timber—roof props, crossbars, and caps— were essential to working the Big Vein coal. The top of the Elk Garden Big Vein seam often had "slips"—wedge-shaped formations—that could collapse unless vertical props were wedged against the roof with cap pieces. Regulations required that hardwood roof props be four inches in diameter and softwood, five; and "timbering" to support the mine roof had to be maintained no more than five to six feet from the face of the coal seam where the miners worked. Whether used for stockade paling, portico column, or mining prop, wood had tremendous adaptability.[32]

In cadence with the swift march of the railroad into the Alleghenies, the introduction of balloon-frame construction made possible the quick creation of mill and coal towns. Framing a house no longer required the use of ponderous mortised, tenoned, and pegged foot-square timbers, as had been the case for thousands of years. Inexperienced workers could easily assemble a balloon-frame house with light two-by-fours and machine-made nails in a fraction of the time.[33] As a consequence, the houses of a mill or coal town would replace an entire mountainside of trees in just several weeks.

Kempton, Maryland, was one such town.

PART TWO

Life in Two Coal Towns

5

Kempton

Have you heard the news from Kempton? Splendid isn't it? Something to be proud of. Kempton, the youngest town of Garrett County; Kempton, a mining town on the Western Maryland Railroad; Kempton, one of the patriotic towns of the county, the town that does things.

—Oakland (Maryland)
Mountain Democrat,
4 July 1918[1]

Closest town to the Fairfax Stone, Kempton was established by the Davis Coal and Coke Company in 1913 to mine the Upper Freeport or Davis vein, the richest in the Upper Potomac Valley. Although Davis Coal and Coke had been founded by Henry Davis, the company had been taken over by the Gould interests in 1905, three years after these same interests had acquired the West Virginia Central.[2]

Kempton was to be a model town, Davis Coal and Coke's showpiece. It was started on a hillside above the Potomac, where a strip of ground was cleared three-quarters of a mile long and several hundred feet wide. The contract for Mine No. 42's twin shafts had been let to a Pittsburgh firm in the summer of 1913; a three-mile freight siding from Wilsonia was ready for service in March 1914, and that September Mine No. 42 was opened for coal shipment. The main hoist house was a brick building with asbestos shingles—''absolutely

The model company town of Kempton, as it looked just before World War I.

fireproof.'' The hoist was driven electrically by a four-hundred-horsepower Allis Chalmer motor. Although No. 42 was producing 250 to 300 tons per day in these first months of operation, the Maryland mine inspector reported that the shaft, when fully developed, would be capable of hoisting 2,000 tons of coal per day. An electrical substation, fan building, blacksmith shop, tool shop, and another hoist house for men and material made up the rest of the mining complex. Thirty-six ''substantial'' houses had been completed and more were on the way.

In the spring of 1915, the Garrett County Board of Education ordered a monthly salary of forty dollars for Kempton's first schoolteacher, J. H. Weimer, and appointed three school trustees. Total enrollment for grades one through seven for the 1916 school year was fifty-three, with a rapid rise to eighty-six in 1917.

Most of Kempton's homes were single-family—four or six rooms each—while only ten were two-family, the type found in most company towns. The superintendent's house was white; all the rest were gray. Each house had a separate lot, enough for a lawn in front and a small garden in the rear. The houses were plank with tile foundations, and since the town was on the side of a hill, every house had a basement. Construction was lath and plaster, with softwood tongue-and-groove flooring and asbestos shingle roofing. The houses had no insulation. Each had a chimney but the miners furnished their own stoves for heating and cooking. Kempton had no indoor plumb-

ing; instead, there was an outhouse for every two houses.[3]

A central power station in Thomas, West Virginia, supplied alternating current. Water was pumped from a ring in the material shaft above the coal measure to a 36,000-gallon tank on the hill behind the town. Gravity feed then carried it to fireplugs and a pull-up spigot in the back between every two houses.

The company store, operated by Buxton and Landstreet Company, was on the west side of town just across the state line in West Virginia. (Company stores were outlawed in Maryland in 1868.)[4] It stocked food, furniture, clothes, mining supplies, and animal feed. Next door was the amusement arcade called the Opera House, with lunchroom, bowling alleys, pool tables, dancing

In Kempton most sidewalks were made of wood. Open ditches carried waste water down the streets.

floor, and an auditorium for plays, lectures, and moving pictures.[5]

Main Street—also known as Front Street and "Kempton Boulevard"—was the only paved street in Kempton, and both the street and its cement sidewalk were points of pride. The "English" lived on Main Street; it was the place to live. The superintendent's house on the corner of Main and Second, across from the Opera House, was the first house a person saw when he drove in town. The manager of the company store lived in the third house on Main, the butcher in the fourth, and the company doctor in the seventh. The foreman or fire boss also lived on Main but at the other end, closest to the mine. Second Street was also prestigious, and its citizens "took pride in their yards."[6]

Pride and Patriotism

Second, Third, Fourth, Fifth, and Sixth streets ran up the hillside. The streets were unpaved and difficult to travel in wet or icy weather. At any given time several factors in a culture will determine which building material is most desirable, but wood seems to have always been universally considered a second-class material for sidewalks. As wooden sidewalks ran beside the streets, the quick echo of his shoe striking the board would remind a citizen that he was not in the best part of town. From time to time boards would disappear from the walks; a person walking at night soon learned where the boards were missing. The company's all-round man responsible for repairs could never find the missing boards, and so one thing seemed certain: if a miner removed a board for one purpose or another—to build a shelf or start a fire—he would never take it from the front of his own house.[7]

Gladys Corbin was twenty-one in 1916 when she and her husband, Claud, moved to Kempton. Gladys was of Welsh extraction, Claud was part Cherokee. The town was still growing and Mine No. 42 was working full tilt, six days a week. The coal produced was "proven...to be first class in every way." There was one bad accident that year, the day after Claud Corbin got his job. This shocked the company and strengthened its determination to make No. 42 one of the safest mines in the region.[8]

Early Kempton was isolated. A shopping trip to Thomas or a longer expedition to Cumberland meant a mile hike for Gladys Corbin—along the boardwalk over the swampy Potomac and up the mountainside to Western Maryland's Beechwood passenger stop. During the summer, primitive trucks and cars could make it in on a rough dirt road. Hucksters came over the rocky route bringing vegetables, meats, cheese, butter, and milk.[9]

If a miner was out of money between paydays, he could get an advance of "chinky-tink," as miners' scrip was known in the region. A dollar of Kempton chinky-tink would bring only seventy-five or eighty cents in Thomas or another town, so a miner felt obliged to do his shopping at Kempton's Buxton and Landstreet. The company store may have had higher prices, but it was just at the edge of town and a miner got full value there for his chinky-tink.[10]

Gladys Corbin built many of her family's meals around twenty-five-pound sacks of flour. Her first baking made ten to twelve loaves of bread; her second, six to eight. A dishpan of cookies was a popular item. The first picking of blackberries from the woods around the town went into cobblers, while the rest was canned. The Corbin youngsters collected apples and huckleberries for

Punched with a "K", this scrip was good only at the company store in Kempton.

The Kempton Boys' Band, 1918.

preserving and crab apples to be spiced. Once the children filled a twenty-five-pound flour sack with mushrooms. Gladys soaked them in salt water and fried them in butter. There were also things from the garden—tomatoes to be canned—and every now and then they'd have fried rabbit. *Our Own People*, the company magazine, related that wild turkey stuffed with oysters was served during the years of World War I.[11]

The war made growing food at home more popular and patriotic; Davis Coal and Coke held a Victory Garden contest, offering three months' free rent as first prize. The best gardens were pictured in *Our Own People*.[12]

During the war years a rising star in the company's management was Mine Superintendent Matthew Stewart. He worked proudly for the company, the town, and the church, and he called on everybody to work together to win the war. In his speech at the 1917 Christmas program, his wish was that each Kempton citizen "be filled with the patriotic as well as the Yuletide spirit.... Every citizen should be proud to march beneath the floating folds of our red, white and blue."[13]

Matt was also the proud color-bearer for the Kempton Boys Band. The band played in Oakland for the War Savings Stamp drive and toured Garrett County for five days with local Republican candidates in October of 1919. The band regularly serenaded Kempton's newlyweds in a town ritual in which the couple was rolled up and down the streets in a wheelbarrow. After five young ladies joined the band, it became the Boys and Girls Band. Enthusiasm to help the group ran high. A lawn social raised $110, and the New Kempton Dramatic Club also did some benefits for the band in Thomas and other neighboring towns.

Matt served as school trustee and Sunday school superintendent. In addition, he headed the company's First Aid Association, and in 1919 the First Aid team won top place in West Virginia.[14]

Matt was also member of several Flag Day committees and was prominent in the festivities in June 1917 when the company gave the town a steel pole for the Flag Day celebration. Young Kempton Adams of New York City presented a great eleven-by-twenty-two-foot American flag, which was raised to the accompaniment of speeches and band music. Kempton had been named after the young man's father, an illustrious banker and owner of Western Maryland Railroad stock. After the speeches,

> everybody broke ranks and hurried over to the schoolhouse, where refreshments were served. Special committees carried refreshments to the sick of Kempton, that they might feel something of the cheer of the day.[15]

In the fall of 1918, nineteen Kempton men were in World War I service. Two died in action. Under Davis Coal and Coke auspices, Private Robert Quigley of the Canadian 19th Battalion spoke to meetings in Kempton and neighboring towns. He explained the construction of trenches, barbed wire entanglements, and listening posts, and he told how getting out the coal was "winning the war."[16] Kempton's Red Cross branch of 152 members made sweaters, bed socks, pajamas, and other hospital needs. It also gave a fund-raising dance in the red-white- and blue-bunted community hall. Then came Armistice Day. The First Aid team formed in front of Buxton and Landstreet and, followed by a happy crowd, carried the image of "Kaiser William" to an appropriate burial.[17]

By 1918 Kempton had 106 houses and a population of 850. The town continued to grow; Buxton and Landstreet expanded, and the company planned 10 more houses. People put their "names on the list for the next group" to be built. *Our Own People* humorously suggested that the newlyweds were causing "all the trouble."[18]

War's end was a time of illness—scarlet fever, membraneous croup, and whooping cough. Gladys and Claud Corbin's second baby, Thelma May, became ill and died when they visited Gladys's parents at Christmas time. Flu swept the town. Fifty cases were reported by January 1919. The mine was paralyzed, and the community building became a hospital. Eight died. Some were buried in the cemetery on Maivies Hill behind the town. Davis Coal and Coke organized medical help for all its mining towns, and one of the recruits who fought the pestilence in Kempton was Dr. George Rowe, an intern from Johns Hopkins Hospital in Baltimore. In April the West Virginia Health Department's railroad car visited the town and gave lessons in preventive health care.[19]

As in all mines, the threat of accident and death was constant in the shadowy work world of No. 42. Youngsters, doing half a turn and getting half pay, soon learned to face the threat, usually working side by side with their fathers. Yet Kempton's mine was considered the safest and most modern in the region when the bad accident occurred. On Tuesday, February 29, 1916, at 6:45 A.M., shortly after the men started work, there was a dust explosion some two thousand feet from the base of the shaft. Seventy-one miners were entombed. Five were seriously injured, and a fall of slate crushed fifteen to death. Those out of range of the blast rushed back to the base of the shaft. Bill Markovitch, manning the hoist, ran the cage up and down as fast as he could, bringing miners to the surface. One man leaped from the hoist, hugged Bill in joy, and kissed the ground.

Damage was not widespread; fans continued to function and rescuers reported the workings practically free of gas. Some wanted to continue to work but without their helmets, and the foreman would not permit it. R.P. Maloney, general superintendent of Davis Coal and Coke, took charge of the hastily organized rescue parties and by Wednesday morning had accounted for everyone. The *Baltimore Sun* reported the accident and aftermath in some detail, but, with reference to the dead, said only that it was impossible to get their names as all were foreigners and working by number. According to the mine inspector's annual report, fourteen were Austrian and one was Italian.[20]

Our Own People pointed out that the two-thirds of the miners who spoke English accounted for only 53 percent of the mining fatalities. A further comment that this was true although 25 percent of those speaking English were "colored" suggests the depth of racial prejudice. In a paper that he read before the Kempton Mining Institute, Dr. L. J. Lanich, company doctor for Kempton, spoke of the matter in another way: "Our average English-speaking miner is a natural born first-aid man."[21] *Our Own People* urged, "stamp out the use of...nicknames...[such as] Dago, Dutchy, Froggy, Ginny, Greaser, Heiny, Howat, Hunky, Kike, Mick, Paddy, Sheeny, Spaghetti, Wop." Nevertheless, Front Street in Kempton was not readily open to the foreigner unless he became a foreman; "hunkies lived on the back streets."[22]

A coal miner's hostile environment argued persuasively for comradeship, regardless of a co-worker's origin. As Dr. Lanich pointed out, "The blast of a mine explosion is a call to every common, work-a-day miner, who will risk his life in the work of rescuing his fellow-miners, as has been proved over and over again." The idea moved him to exhortation:

> One person in a community with civic interest in his heart, proves the force of the individual. We are all parts of a whole. Not one of us can live his life away from other lives and lead a rich full life....It is the day of the slogan: "Each for the other and all together."[23]

Such was the spirit and optimism of Kempton's leaders at the end of the decade.

6
Prosperity and Problems

*Our little mining town of Kempton, usually
so quiet and peaceful, has experienced a series
of thrills that would make an inhabitant of
wicked Chicago sit up and take notice.*

—Oakland (Maryland) Republican,
10 April 1924[1]

There were times in the twenties when the people of
Kempton seemed to be squarely divided—some in the
camp of the devil, and others in the camp of the Lord.

Although Kempton never had a church, it never
lacked for religious activity. "Old time" revival meetings
were common. One of them, conducted by the Reverend
Mr. Puffenbarger on the theme of sin and salvation,
lasted for eight weeks in the late winter of 1922. The
theater and the schoolhouse were used regularly for services and Sunday school; the flagpole circle near the mine
tipple was used for one outdoor revival.

Among the Protestants, Methodists predominated.
The Parent-Teachers Association, which raised $115 for
the school, also donated $60 to the Methodist preacher,
with nary a concern that somebody might object, and
in fact nobody did. The few members of the Church of
God met in the miners' homes.[2] Catholics, many of
whom were foreign-born (Italians, Poles, Greeks, Lithu-
anians), carpooled to Thomas for Mass. Father Spiller
gave instructions at the Kempton schoolhouse on occasion, but parents also drove young people to Thomas

for Confraternity of Christian Doctrine (CCD) instruction before their first communion and confirmation.[3]

But organized religion was not the only force that attempted to influence the morality of Kempton's citizens. The Ku Klux Klan, which gathered up numbers of disciples in eastern and central United States in the mid-twenties, was active though short-lived in Kempton. As in other communities, opposition to foreigners, Catholics, and Negroes was not necessarily the Klan's sole concern. Although there were black miners in the region, none lived or worked in Kempton; it is said the only colored who came into town found himself unwelcome and left the same day.* A primary aim of the Klan was to keep those its leaders identified as troublemakers in line or, as some of them put it, to maintain community values.

A wave of moonshining triggered Klan crusading in 1924. At 10:30 one April morning George Hawkins, federal enforcement officer from Cumberland, swept into town with two assistants. He speedily deputized ten citizens and in three hours raided ten houses—10 percent of all the homes in Kempton—and made ten arrests. The morning's work uncovered twelve stills, a hundred gallons of liquor, and eight hundred gallons of mash. The stills were easily found, and it was quite a haul. The agents took the suspects to Cumberland. Three finally got off with one dollar fines, while six received five days each in the county jail. Newspapers reported that the men were all foreigners and worked as miners when not engaged in the manufacture of moonshine.[4]

The night after the raid, dynamite explosions split the air, and a great cross burned on the hill to the south of town. Later that April, the Reverend Mr. Elkins, the revivalist, was holding extended meetings in the movie theater. At the start of one service, eight hooded Klansmen entered, silently advanced to the altar, laid fifty

---

*According to Roy Gibbs, when on one occasion the Davis Company tried to haul coal underground into No. 42 from an adjoining mine at Pierce, West Virginia, that employed black miners, the Kempton miners went on strike.

dollars on the table, and left as quietly as they had come. Then a day or two after the cross burning, an "undesirable citizen" was escorted to the company office, given the pay due him, and advised to leave town.[5]

But neither federal agents nor Klansmen apparently dampened the energy and industry of Kempton bootleggers, whose stills had been making wine and beer as well as moonshine. By the end of August there was another raid. At seven in the morning, Prohibition Agent J. L. Asher, Jr., from Washington descended on the town with two deputies in a "high-powered car." By one o'clock they had visited fifteen homes. While it was conjectured that a number of residents had been tipped off and hid their stills, six were arrested. In one house the agents found wife and son in the act of pouring out the mash. The penetrating pungent odor lingered around the miners' houses for some days. During the raid Deputy Luther Hopwood said that he heard nine different languages; newspaper headlines pointed out that all arrested were foreign-born.[6]

With the flurry of these mid-twenties events, the *Oakland Republican* reported that Davis Coal and Coke was "encouraging all legitimate activities and amusements." The old Kempton band was revived and a men's basketball team organized. Radio increasingly became a medium for entertainment, and the newspaper commented on the fine quality of the shows on Saturday nights at the movie theater.[7]

Meanwhile, new arrivals came to work in the mine, and there were never enough houses. One of the newcomers, Italian-born Frank Anthony Carbone, arrived with his family in 1924 when he was ten. The Carbones were a poor, close-knit Catholic family, and the parents were strict; the children had to be home at nine sharp. Italian was spoken in the home, and since Catherine, the mother, did not know English, the rest of the family did the grocery shopping. Catherine was a good cook, her husband a good gardener. Like those of many of the foreigners, their home was up on the hill on a back street, and like most of their neighbors they kept pigs and a cow.[8]

57

Another new resident in the twenties was Dr. E. E. Sollars, who took over as company doctor in the summer of 1929. The son of a farmer, Dr. Sollars went to Charlotte Hall Academy in southern Maryland. He taught school for two years, found it dull, and switched to medicine at Maryland Medical College. An account in the *Glades Star* tells how, after interning at Franklin Square, "one of the finest hospitals" in Baltimore, he hung out his shingle in June of 1910. When he became company doctor, his wife and children stayed in Deer Park, where he would go on the weekends. He charged ten dollars for delivering a baby, and fifteen dollars if a nurse was to provide maternity care. (One couple who saved up the money kept it under the living room rug until they worried that someone would notice the bulge, whereupon they changed the ones to a single ten.) A coat and tie were standard dress for Doctor Sollars, a felt hat when appropriate, and he never sat down for a meal without putting on his suit coat, upholding the dignity of his profession in a company coal town. He also had a warm and friendly smile.

Clinics in Dr. Sollars's office, like those in other company towns, were an efficient means of delivering health care. Dr. Folk of Cumberland conducted successful dental clinics, and Dr. Bess of Keyser conducted once-a-year clinics for adenoids and tonsils, at which he usually operated on from twelve to fifteen children. After the youngsters recovered from anesthesia, mothers were instructed "to get a pint of ice cream and take 'em home."[9]

It was 1926 when Elmer Clark and his stepfather moved to Kempton. Elmer, known as Gooch to his friends, was born in Morgantown in 1911. He was in grammar school when he first came to Kempton, and in 1928 he became a member of the first class at the new high school.* He went to Sunday school in Thomas—

*Garrett County's superintendent of schools and Governor Nice himself had led the move for Kempton High, the sixth high school in Garrett County. Kempton citizens took great pride in their high school. The first class insisted they have a full-scale graduation— banquet, class night, and commencement with a baccalaureate, valedictory, and a Board of Education member as speaker.[10]

Kempton grade school, 1925.

to all three as a matter of fact (Presbyterian, Methodist, and Church of the Brethren), which the staggered hours of services enabled him to do. Young people coveted the bronze, silver, and gold badges for good attendance. Elmer received the gold badge and wouldn't have traded it for the biggest farm in Texas. Although short of stature, he could "run like a deer," a talent that particularly caught the attention of Asa Lewis, principal of the new high school.[11]

Principal Asa Lewis was forty-one the year he and Edna, his wife of two years, moved to Kempton from Kitzmiller, where he had been principal. Studious as a young man, he had attended West Virginia Wesleyan. The draft interrupted college, but he took advantage of a World War I GI bill to study at Toulouse. Service in France gave him a chance to travel—to see the Roman amphitheater at Nimes, to visit Lourdes and the French Alps, and to hear President Wilson give the 1919 Memorial Day address to the troops at Paris. For several summers when the Lewises lived in Kempton, Asa studied at West Virginia University and earned his M.A. Their house was the last on Second Street, next to the Potomac, and fourth down from the mine superintendent's. Here their three children were born, and here they lived until 1948, when the high school was merged with Oakland.

During 1928-29, Kempton High's beginning year, classes were held in the doctor's office on Front Street. Besides serving as principal, Asa Lewis taught the first-year class.

Asa also took a strong interest in field day, the annual statewide athletic event in which Kempton never took less than second place. Elmer Clark's fleetness of foot would have made him a sure winner, and Asa urged him to get tennis shoes. When Elmer's father refused to buy them, Asa said he would buy the shoes for him, but Elmer wouldn't let him.[12]

Even though the larger mines could operate fairly constantly, times were no longer easy in the Maryland coal towns. In the twenty years ending in 1929—a few years longer than No. 42 had been shipping coal—the major coal-burning industries had increased their efficiency by a third and demand was down. With the depression deepening and the need for more family income pressing in, Elmer Clark left high school and went to work in No. 42.[13]

7
Tough Times and Political Strife

Oh! yes there were times when
the mines were slack

The men would walk down
the railroad track

To search for greens and
berries too

Often a whistle pig [a woodchuck]
helped make the stew.

—"The Town That Used To Be,"
by Ida Geroski, miner's widow
and former resident of Kempton

The depression years made it difficult for boys to finish high school. Tony Carbone dropped out in 1930 and started to work in the mine. However, there were no steady jobs and work was erratic; from the early thirties until World War II, a miner often worked only one day a week in No. 42.

Two years after Tony started to work, his father was badly hurt, the side of his face cut open and his back broken. Compensation came to six dollars a week. Tony took care of six younger brothers and sisters and his mother. Some mornings there was no work but, though most of the others went home, Tony would wait around the mine, hoping that a job might turn up and that they would need a man for the rest of the day. At one time or another he filled just about every job—motorman, brakeman, coal loader. It was a hard life held together with the fiber of strong family ways. After work, he would take his bath in a large boiler tub in the back of the house. His mother heated the water on the stove and always had his clean clothes and dinner waiting.[1]

Stanley Turek moved to Kempton in '29. One of nine children, he was born in Albert, Virginia, in 1908. The Tureks kept to the customs of the Old World. Sauerkraut with Polish sausage was a staple, and every year Stanley performed the ritual task of stamping the sauerkraut in a great barrel. But people kidded the parents for keeping such old ways, and the Tureks discarded them with shame.

As Stanley grew up, events and needs moved the family from place to place in the West Virginia coal fields. Adrian was a bad town; housewives couldn't even hang out the laundry because of the smoky coke ovens. The Tureks stayed only six months, leaving before winter came. Then, in Benbush, when a company spy told him to keep his son away from the union meetings, Stanley's father got mad and they moved to still another town.

Stanley had learned about unions early, having hauled food in his wagon to the men on the picket line in Henry when the family lived there in 1922. It felt good to be part of the struggle against the company. Shortly thereafter, though his father disapproved, he dropped out of school (he was then in the eighth grade) and went to work in the mine.

The depression days of 1932 were particularly tough. The Maryland Bureau of Mines reported that coal companies remitted rental on company houses, divided the available jobs among the miners, and extended credit at the company stores. Twenty-three-year-old Stanley Turek and his wife had a baby boy at a time when the available food could hardly be called infant fare: "whistle pigs"—woodchucks shot in nearby meadows—or "potatoes and beans, potatoes and beans," as the depression food litany went in the mining towns. No. 42 had worked only one day in the last month, and in desperation Stanley and a friend, Burnie Broll, went into Buxton and Landstreet looking for credit to buy milk. When it looked as if they were going to be refused, one of them (Stanley can't remember who) said something to the effect that if they couldn't get it any other way, they'd "blow the place up!" Knowing that the men usually had dynamite for mining, the company reacted quickly. Two state police and a "company thug"—a Davis Coal and Coke safety officer—were brought into town. After a quick conference the company gave every Kempton miner six dollars credit at the company store.[2]

Relief also came from outside Kempton. The Red Cross, the Quakers, and the Hoover Committee sent clothes and food. The school children had raisins and cocoa in a free school lunch. Powdered milk, beans, and butter were distributed. Flour was sent in by boxcar. Stanley Turek helped unload the flour but received no favored treatment for his work. Garrett County provided free seed for vegetable gardens through the company store, but with dubious results since the miners had to buy their own fertilizer.

Davis Coal and Coke asked Asa Lewis, Dr. Sollars, and Gilbert P. Smith, manager of the company store, to serve as a committee for the distribution of relief goods. The job had its problems. For one thing, when old shoes were passed out, proper sizes were not always available. This created tensions and resentments, and Edna Lewis felt badly about the hard feelings. Maxine, one of the Corbin girls, hated the blue-and-black striped flannel that was distributed for clothes. It was a bad time, and there were occasions when the housewives cussed out the clerk at Buxton and Landstreet.[3]

Competition from other power sources exacerbated the distress. *Davis Coal News*, a trade journal, appeared in the early thirties to extol the merits of coal—the "basic fuel...upon which every major industry depends."[4] The magazine featured pictures of facilities at No. 42—the tipple, the picking table, and the interior of the mine. While proposing more efficient uses of coal, it mustered arguments against the use of other fuels: federal geologists had warned a congressional committee that unless production was curbed, the nation's oil reserves would

The tipple at Kempton.

be exhausted by 1949;[5] the coal industry was being sacrificed to the "grandiose program and ruinous policy of Federal water power development";[6] and "exhaust from an oil burner...pollutes the sweet spring air."[7]

The hard times brought a change in the political wind. Although Garrett County had always been rock-ribbed Republican, the laboring men—particularly the miners—were moving to Franklin Roosevelt. Hoover carried the county with a good 57 percent of the vote in '32, but of the 142 votes in Kempton, 48 percent were for Hoover, 44 percent for Roosevelt, and 8 percent for Norman Thomas, the Socialist candidate. In subsequent elections Roosevelt won easily in Kempton even though the Republicans swept the county better than two to one. The Kempton tally in 1944 was Roosevelt and Truman, 111; Dewey and Bricker, 53. The mining towns of Kitzmiller and Vindex were also strongly Democratic.[8]

Edna Lewis remembers election days as the noisiest of the year. Kempton's polling place was in Dr. Sollars's office, and there was considerable drinking and carrying on. When a voter approached, the campaign worker would call out, "Give you a drink if you vote for Roosevelt." In the context of Kempton, this was surely one of the more superfluous political promises in American history.

When the new administration started the Civilian Conservation Corps, three of the Corbin boys joined up.[9] The New Deal atmosphere supported a stronger union movement. As Gladys Corbin said, "Roosevelt straightened them out and let the Union back in." The passage of the Norris-LaGuardia Act in 1933 meant that the so-called Yellow Dog or company union contract—an agreement not to organize—was no longer binding. That year organizers and miners met twice in the apple orchard on the hill behind the town. The company had spies there and the union organizers knew who they were, but there were no hard feelings. Then Davis Coal and Coke called a meeting in the recreation hall and asked for a vote on staying in the Yellow Dog Union. But the miners wanted their own union. They shouted, raised their hands, and—there was no doubt about it—United Mine Workers Local 4113 was on its way.[10]

Another group organized in January of 1933. "Pastor Reverend" Chamberlain led the women in founding a Ladies Aid Society, and Edna Lewis was its first president. Its activities often had a charitable dimension. Bazaars, candy and bake sales, and socials raised money for good works, such as providing clothes for commencement exercises for students of needy families. Cultural betterment was a regular part of each meeting's program. Among the books covered by the reading chairman's periodic reviews were *How Green Was My Valley; Listen, the Wind; Lee of Virginia; Highland Heritage; All This, and Heaven Too;* and *River Supreme.* Hymns, Scripture readings, and Bible contests filled the fourth Friday monthly meetings; "Climb though the Rocks be Rugged" was the motto.

During the thirties and forties, from five to thirty

women attended the meetings of the Ladies Aid Society (sometime in the forties, it became the Women's Society of Christian Services). Some were also members of the Homemakers Club and over the years held several offices in each club. Most of the club leaders lived in the "downtown" section on Front Street or in the new section where Edna and Asa Lewis lived, between Front and the Potomac. On occasion some of the officers would collect dues from members when they shopped at Buxton and Landstreet. But Edna Lewis never approved of this, and Asa agreed with her.[11]

Ethel Fox was another of Kempton's leading club women. The Foxes had come to Kempton in '34. They were a big family—three girls and four boys. Asa Lewis helped the oldest daughter, as he helped others, to attend college at Mountain Lake Park. The mother was always doing things for other families, and it became a family joke that whenever she baked a cake or pie, the children wanted to know, "Who is it for this time?" The Foxes couldn't afford a newspaper, so much of Ethel's information on current events came from the University of Maryland's Homemakers Office. She attended the annual university week-long homemaking courses for club women from around the state. Ethel also held offices and chairmanships in the Homemakers and the Women's Society for several years.[12]

In October 1938, when she was president of the Homemakers, Ethel suggested that the club write to President Roosevelt and thank him for his part in bringing about the Munich Conference. Ethel appointed Edna Lewis and Mrs. Lewis Duling, wife of the Buxton and Landstreet butcher, to write the letter. The Homemakers also had a peace chairman and subscribed to literature from the Women's International League for Peace and Freedom.* However, they were bothered by charges that

*The Women's International League for Peace and Freedom (WILPF) was founded in 1915 by Jane Addams, founder of Hull-House and an ardent pacifist. WILPF works for total disarmament and the elimination of war through nonviolent means, urges the end of discrimination on any basis, and supports the transfer of funds from the military budget to human needs.

peace organizations were a fraud, and in the last months of 1939 there was some disagreement among the women as to whether they should continue the club's subscription.[13]

In 1939 Stanley Turek was elected union president for No. 42 and subsequently was reelected for two more one-year terms. Union meetings were held every Saturday at one o'clock and lasted about an hour. A major concern was improving safety conditions. Under the contract the miners had to take their grievances to the company before they could bring them to the union. It was especially hard to get the foreigners to follow this procedure because they were afraid to complain to their foreman. Life was difficult enough for the immigrant worker without inviting retaliation.**

There was generally a thirty-day strike before the annual contract was renewed. On many a morning during these strikes, Stanley would be awakened to pull two or three men off the job, for despite the strike several men persisted in trying to get in a day's work fixing mine carts or working at the picking table.[14]

Whether there was a strike or the mine was closed, idle time in Kempton was slow and tedious. It was spent playing cards by the hour, sitting outside Buxton and Landstreet, walking down the tracks for a bottle of moonshine, or hunting for a rabbit or a whistle pig.

And there was idle time for the family. After Sunday school one Mother's Day, Ethel Lewis found the afternoon very dull. She made potato salad and baked one of her favorite recipes, whole wheat muffins. The family walked along the creek-sized Potomac and picnicked under the trees by some pinkies near a patch of ramps.

But in the world of the Kempton youngster there was never idle time. The springtime ramp, a favorite West

---

**Roy Wiseman of Elk Garden tells how a miner's patronage of the company store regulated his working conditions. If the miner spent all his earnings at the store, he would receive all the cars he could load (cars were often in short supply in the mines). If he didn't spend most of his money in the store, he would be put in a "dip" or wet place to work. If he continued to be uncooperative, he would be blacklisted.

Children playing dodge ball.

Virginia leek gathered from marshy spots, was ideal leverage to obtain dismissal from school and freedom for games. A youngster who had eaten ramps would exude from every pore a vapor more potent and penetrating than that of any onion; for anyone close by, such an atmosphere made study impossible. Ramps secretly rubbed on the hot stove on a cool April day could make the whole classroom unfit for human habitation.

The games and pastimes were the universal pleasures of boyhood. The boys played cops-and-robbers with "uptowners" and "downtowners" on competing sides. (When a robber escaped across the Maryland-West Virginia boundary, which ran through the edge of town, he was safe from arrest.) They also played war, shooting choke cherries at the enemy through the hollow stems of joe-pye weed. The BB-like fruit really hurt.

Autumn days were spent gathering apples and berries, with an extravaganza of maple and oak color for a backdrop. In the winter there was sleigh riding with stops at Dr. Sollars's office afterwards to get warm by his stove. Though his hands shook a little, Dr. Sollars could be counted on to treat each youngster to a spoonful of sugary cough medicine.[15]

The years in Kempton for Edna and Asa Lewis were difficult. They didn't have much of a house—Edna joked that her feet were perpetually cold in the winter—and the depression was tough. But the Kempton years were the best times: here their three children—Lynn, Marshall, and Elaine—were born and here they had a happy home.[16]

Tough Times

8
Wartime and Winding Down

*I've been working for 26 years: the only job
I've ever had. There's no work at the other
mines. The company offered me my 4-room
house for $2,200 some time ago. With no job,
what good is that house on the hill?*

— Kempton miner in the
Baltimore Evening Sun,
12 May 1950[1]

The club leaders' concern with war and peace continued into the troubled forties. In March of 1942 the
Homemakers (Edna Lewis was president that year) finally disapproved paying dues to the Women's International League for Peace and Freedom. Nevertheless,
the club appointed a peace chairman, Ethel Fox, for
1943, and she served as peace chairman again in 1944,
when one of her programs was a discussion of the Atlantic
Charter. The women increased their support of the war
effort, offering *Reader's Digest* subscriptions for Kempton servicemen, promoting various Red Cross projects,
and holding club discussions on such subjects as hoard-
ing, child labor safeguards, wartime diets and sacrifices,
and the defense of democracy and its free institutions.[2]

Kempton raised no money for the 1942 USO drive,

but the sixth- and seventh-grade boys filled a large room at school for the scrap drive. The February 1942 Selective Service Registration had signed up thirty-seven Kempton men between the ages of twenty and forty-four; the July registration tallied nineteen between the ages of eighteen and twenty. During the rest of the year seven young men from Kempton were among Garrett County inductees.[3]

That same year, the Garrett County superintendent of schools announced that Kempton High was to close. Henceforth, the forty to forty-five students would attend improved educational facilities in Thomas, West Virginia. Not only would the county save money, but "the change had the approval of the people of Kempton and . . . [the] president of the Davis Coal and Coke Company," which had a mine in Thomas as well. Wanda Corbin was in the last graduating class of four girls and three boys. After graduation, she went to work in Buxton and Landstreet with her sister Maxine. The Lewises moved to Oakland, where Asa became principal of Oakland High. As a show of affection the Kempton Homemakers honored Edna with a farewell dinner at Backbone Mountain Inn.[4]

Wartime demand for coal was on the increase, and Elmer Clark, who was now married, put in as much time in the mine as he could. He and his wife, Twila, had four children, and a fifth was on the way. The money anxiety was strong. Even though coal production was up, it was still a rarity to put in a full week in the mine, and sometimes you were lucky to get even two or three days.

On July 10 of that summer, Dr. Sollars was caring for Twila as well as for her neighbor, Vermelda Kurcaba, both of whom were in labor and near delivery. Fortunately, the two lived close together in the row of double houses. Doc Sollars was keeping the "boardwalk hot," hurrying back and forth between them; the two babies were going to arrive within minutes of each other. Vermelda's delivery was easy, but when Doc hastened back to Twila's, he found a frightened midwife: the infant was emerging feet first—a breech birth. Doc took

Doc Sollars.

over. With all but the head delivered, his experienced hands executed a twist and the birth was complete. The Clark's fifth was a fine seven-pound boy.

Doc Sollars was strict in keeping with conservative obstetrical practice of the day. As it was, miners' wives had little chance to rest, although orders were to stay in bed a full ten days after delivery, with no getting up and walking. Elmer wanted to stay home the next day to mind the house and family, but there was a chance to work on the A.M. shift and that was hard to ignore. Though Clara, the oldest child, was ten, she wasn't up to handling the other children. Twila insisted that she could manage; if she needed to she could knock on the wall and get help from the neighbor in the other half of the double house.

With all this indecision Elmer was late. He had no time for breakfast. He jammed some food and a water bottle into his lunch pail and sprinted down the walk toward the mine. It was still pretty dark. His foot caught on a board, he sprawled, and food, water bottle, and pail went everywhere. Stuffing them back together, he raced onto the mine hoist just in time. Catching the hoist was a break. He could have caught it on the next trip down, but the mine train would have already left from the foot of the shaft, and he would have had to hike a mile and a quarter to his work place. As the hoist descended, he used the water running down the side of the shaft to wash out his pail and refill the bottle.

Pushed and hurried, he didn't fill out a report on the conditions in the work area. His first job on the shift was to move the cutting machine from the crosscut and start it up the main heading. A roof prop was in the way, and he started to knock the cap off the prop. It had been a morning of distractions, but he didn't think he was too hasty in not providing another support in place of the prop; he felt the roof would hold. He knocked out the cap. Instantly, a boulder dropped from the roof onto his leg and pinned him to the floor. His crew pried the rock off.

Almost any man with a broken leg would not try to move, and he probably would be in some degree of shock. But excitement seized Elmer and he started crawling for the conveyor. One way or another he wanted to get out of the mine. His crew pulled him back, got him to lie down, and tore away his pant leg to see the extent of the injury. The miners tried to keep him from looking at his broken leg, but he insisted; it wasn't too painful. One of the miners had some tea, and it was just about the best thing that Elmer ever tasted.

They loaded him on a stretcher for the trip out. But two train wrecks on the main heading made interminable delays and detours, and it took four long hours and half a pack of cigarettes to get him to the top of the shaft. Doc Sollars and an ambulance were waiting. Elmer asked the doctor to be sure and tell Twila that the break was a simple fracture and she should not worry.

Ten-year-old Clara Clark saw the ambulance head up Front Street for the Elkins Hospital. She ran to her mother and said she was just certain that Daddy was in that ambulance. With a day-old baby and a house full of children, Twila had plenty to think about. She told Clara that she was sure it wasn't Daddy.

Dr. Sollars forgot to tell Twila about the accident, much less that the injury was not severe, but, as she told her friends, she got back at him. When he came to see her on the tenth day after the delivery, she had gone to Elkins to see Elmer; "Lord o'lipshun," Doc exlaimed.

Elmer was out of work for six and a half months. Workmen's compensation was hardly enough to keep him in cigarettes. The Clarks scraped along somehow, and once he had healed they could only be grateful that the injury had been no worse. If that boulder had struck his leg just a fraction of an inch differently, he'd have been stiff legged and limping the rest of his life.[5]

Early in the forties the union's Pit Committee complained to the company that Stanley Turek and some of the other men were getting sick. It had something to do with the clouds of sand thrown up by the wheels of the electric mine machines that hauled the coal. No. 42 was notorious for its steep tunnels, and with up to an 18 percent grade in some spots, it was necessary to spread sand repeatedly for traction. In response, the company sold the men respirators.

Stanley wanted to be relieved as a motor operator, but the foreman refused. He said that Stanley would be all right; he just didn't drink enough whiskey. When the X rays came back positive for silicosis, the company told the men they would recover if they left mining. Stanley went to work for Bethlehem Steel in Baltimore, but the trouble continued. Eventually, with the help of an attorney, he got a settlement from Davis Coal and Coke.[6]

Still, Kempton had the most modern and best-equipped mine in Maryland. While the majority of Upper Potomac basin mines used mules, No. 42 used eight General Electric mine machines for haulage. Two one-hundred-horsepower pumps, each pumping as much as a thousand gallons a minute, brought drainage water to the surface. A giant electric fan supplied ventilation.[7]

No. 42 was partially mined by pick, but from the mid-twenties on, electric cutters, like those Elmer Gooch Clark used, were employed almost exclusively. Whether made by pick or machine, the undercuts were four to five inches wide and about fifteen feet long, and they ran six feet deep into the base of the seam. Cutting out the "bug dust"—that is, machine-cut coal—wasn't easy. The machine would catch fire, blow a fuse, or break on a sulfur ball, which could vary from the size of an egg to the size of a football. Sometimes the cable had to be repaired. After undercutting the coal, the miner placed explosive in holes drilled along the top of the seam. Only certain types of explosives were permitted in some mines; these "permissible" explosives with special slow-burning qualities were less likely to ignite gas or coal dust when blasting the coal down.* Elmer didn't always go the required one hundred feet before igniting the charge, and so fragments of blasted coal often struck him just like BBs.[8]

By 1944 Kempton's large families were prominent on the Parents Honor Roll for Garrett County. Six Kempton families had three sons each in the service. A seventh had two sons and a daughter. The Charles Millers had four children in the service, as did widow Jennie Ryan.[9]

Widow Ryan's family was a large one: five sons, three in the army, and two daughters, one in cadet nurse training. Jim Ryan had won the Garrett County Marbles Tournament when he was thirteen, and Scripps Howard Papers had sponsored his trip to the National Tournament at Ocean City. A 1934 graduate of Kempton High, he worked a year in No. 42 before entering the service. On May 22, 1944, the army announced that Pfc James Ryan had been killed somewhere in Italy.[10] He was Kempton's first casualty of World War II.

In October Pfc Dale H. Duling was killed somewhere in France. Dale had been a student at Frostburg State and a member of Alpha Sigma. Maxine Corbin took care of the Buxton and Landstreet meat counter for Dale's dad the day word came.[11]

---

*Although more dangerous than the "permissible" explosives, dynamite and black powder were more powerful and therefore often preferred by the miners. Black powder also was inexpensive.

19 40

Kempton High School
Seniors & Faculty

W. Va Photo Co.
Parsons, W.Va.

Kempton High, class of 1940. Top row: Olive Shillingburg, Mildred Raines, Vaude Wolfe, Betty Geroski, Eva Cook, and Nettie Smith. Middle: John Havran, Robert Sprague (teacher), Bill Ryan, Asa Lewis (principal), and Norma Bowers. Bottom: Gene Wilson, Lloyd Greathouse, Jimmy Dice, and Jimmy Gibbs.

During the war No. 42 ran three shifts and overtime, and it was difficult to get enough miners. Young men were drawn away by both war industries and the armed services. Times were better and money was freer. Dr. Sollars left his job with Davis and started a practice in Oakland. As usual, Kempton didn't have enough houses. Some miners lived in Thomas, Pierce, or Ben bush and drove to Kempton. Others came from Henry, trudging to work three and a half miles along the Western Maryland tracks. It was a long walk in the bitter cold of winter.[12]

With the end of the war Kempton children once again marched up and down the streets, beat pans, and shouted. The veterans returned. Men were still needed in the mine, so it was easy to get a job, particularly if one was a good ball player. The union was working hard to build up the Kempton team.[13]

In 1947, Maxine Corbin left her job at the company store to marry Adam Repetsky, a veteran paratrooper. The Repetskys were Catholics and the Corbins Methodists, but the two were married in a Lutheran church. Though born in Henry, Adam spoke Lithuanian, his parents' native tongue. Maxine learned to cook some of the native dishes, especially the two that were Adam's favorites—cabbage soup and hot potatoes dipped in beet soup.[14]

About the time the Repetskys were married, work started to slack off in mine No. 42. For several years, under the pressure of competition, Davis Coal and Coke had been making substantial improvements. In '45 the company installed mechanical loaders; a 30,000-dollar, 17,000-foot conveyor; and drainage pipes lined with acid-resistant material, running from the pump room at the base of the 420-foot shaft to the surface. In '46 the management constructed a million-dollar slate and ash washing plant. By '47, when machines were cutting all of Kempton's coal, the mine reached its peak annual production. But increased efficiency was of no avail. Demand sagged and production costs rose. Labor costs grew, too. The company was paying thirty cents for every ton of coal into the United Mine Worker's Welfare and Pension Fund, and wages had doubled in ten years, from seven dollars a day in 1940 to fourteen dollars and seventy-five cents a day in 1950. The union pressed the coal companies for additional improvements, particularly indoor plumbing in company-owned houses, pointing out among other things that open house drains in Kempton had created sanitary problems in the school yard. Shortly thereafter, Davis Coal and Coke sold its Kempton houses to a Pittsburgh real estate firm.

In March 1950, Manor Coal Mine No. 3—second in Garrett County to No. 42—closed. Manor No. 3's president pointed out that three of their big customers were turning away from coal. Public Service of New Jersey was using oil in 90 percent of its outlets; Consolidated Edison had cut its demand by five million tons a year and was using 60 percent oil. Closest to home, Western

Maryland Railroad was putting fourteen diesels into service and—to add insult to injury—was using them to haul coal trains from western Maryland.

Nevertheless, it came as a shock when the company announced that Mine No. 42 would cease operations at midnight on April 15, 1950. Pete Corbin had always said that the mine would close some day, but nobody believed him. There was still a lot of coal in No. 42, and Davis Coal and Coke had just spent many thousands in improvements. But the shutdown was real, and one by one Kempton's other vital signs disappeared. On April 21 a representative of the Maryland Unemployment Board appeared at the Kempton School to accept claims from more than two hundred Kempton unemployed. The only work left to do—the maintenance of salvage equipment—was being done by a crew of seventy. And after April 21 the company doctor stopped keeping office hours and making house calls. Buxton and Landstreet closed. The clerks threw the Kempton scrip into the bottom of No. 42's shaft.

The Maryland mine shutdown made good copy; the *Oakland* (Maryland) *Republican*, the *Cumberland Times*, the *Baltimore Evening Sun*, and the *Washington Star* had extensive news and feature coverage of No. 42 and other beleaguered mines. Only 115 miners out of 1500 were still at work in Garrett County.[15] The Kempton miners told reporters they couldn't understand the shutdowns and expressed their "fondness" for No. 42. George Sowers, who had mined for twenty-four years, expressed their bitterness most succinctly: "They ought to build a gas chamber for us old bucks and finish us off."[16]

The Pittsburgh real estate firm that bought the houses was now trying unsuccessfully to sell them. Their starting price was $2200 to $2700, but there was little interest. Finally, no more than twelve families made purchases. Maxine and Adam Repetsky got their house for $400; it was the house in which the Corbin children had grown up. The rest of the homes were torn down, hauled away, and sold for lumber. Fortunately, the lights didn't go out; electric power continued to come from Thomas.[17]

The Faces of Kempton

A Portfolio of Photographs by John Vachon

In May 1939, photographer John Vachon arrived to add Kempton to the Farm Security Administration's enlarging documentary of rural and smalltown America. The coal miners were on a thirty-day strike, as they customarily were every year just before their annual contract came up for renewal. Vachon's instructions, however, were to cover the strike not as a news event but as a recurrent episode in the lives of the people. On the pages that follow is his visual report of that episode.

For more about Vachon, see page 167.

Striking coal miners in front of the company store
Paul Arnold, Vergil Miller, Elmer Clark, Gary Serifs

George Montgomery
"Preacher"

Passing time

Family

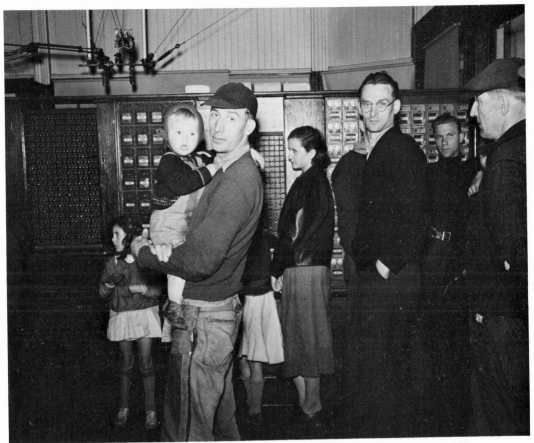

Waiting for the mail

George Blizzard, miner

Mrs. George Blizzard and children

Brother and sister; children of
Mr. and Mrs. George Blizzard

Salvaging coal from a slag pile

Muriel Broll and son Richard

Gertrude Dragovich,
Mike Dragovich,
and Nellie Lewis

Mr. and Mrs. Dragovich

9
Indian Summer

NOTICE OF PROPOSED ABANDONMENT

Notice is hereby given that the Interstate Commerce Commission is being requested...

The reasons for the proposed abandonment are as follows:

There are no shippers or consignees located on the Kempton Branch. Since April 1968, when coal mining operations on the Branch ceased, it has handled no traffic whatsoever. Nor is there any prospect for any future use of the Branch by the shipping public...

— Western Maryland Railway Company,
6 October 1975
[Notice posted in Kempton]

Although the elementary school opened again in the fall of 1950 with thirty-seven students in grades one through ten, Kempton was disappearing. The next April, families of only eighteen of the children were planning to stay. The school closed that fall and the remaining children were bused to Oakland.

The Garrett County Board of Education gave the school patrons the playground equipment and a piano, twelve chairs, one brown bookcase, one stove, one coal bucket, one shovel, one broom, and one dustpan for the

Sunday school. The patrons offered to return the piano and the playground equipment, but the board in far-off Oakland was attentive; it felt that an isolated handful of miners' children might benefit if the items remained. The equipment finally ended up in the school attended by Kempton children at a nearby village, Red House.

The PTA had assisted with school lunches for several years. With No. 42 shut down, the USDA started to provide families with dried milk, potatoes, and dried eggs from the Surplus Food program.[1]

Fortunately, there were spring jobs on the county roads and some seasonal farm work. The superintendent helped Pete Corbin get a job. Pete's son-in-law, Adam Repetsky, used the GI bill to go to barber's school for a year in 1951; after that he barbered in the evening and worked in nearby mines whenever he could during the day.

In 1975 Adam developed cancer and underwent surgery. He hung on as long as he could and wouldn't let them take his name off the company payroll. But it finally got the best of him. After he died, Maxine and the children continued to live in their house, No. 27. She had grown up in this house and had spent all her life in Kempton.[2]

Third baseman Dick Broll, who had "dropped steel" —moving hopper cars after they were loaded—and worked the picking table in No. 42, found work in Cleveland along with some of the men from other coal towns nearby. For six years he worked for Ohio Sheet Metal Die Company. Then, about the time of President Eisenhower's second term, the "roof fell in." There were no jobs. He cooked in a Howard Johnson in Akron for a year and then found a job back in Cleveland again. But Dick never cared for the city. He was one of a group of men who, whenever they could, would drive all the way back to Kempton—just to be back. When he retired, he lived with his widowed mother on the lower side of Front Street.[3]

Stanley Turek's nephew, Walter "Skeeter" Turek, and his wife had a second home on the other side of Front Street from the Brolls. Though born in Kempton,

Skeeter never worked in No. 42 but did work in nearby mines. Here he and his wife could relax. He liked to hunt and drive the mountain roads in his jeep. Fond of animals, he fed pears to the deer on the hill behind the town. Once he had a pet bear, which got out of hand and tore the seat out of his pants.[4]

By December 1952 Western Maryland workers had removed the three miles of rail line into Kempton. The Interstate Commerce Commission had authorized the abandonment the summer before. But when coal-stripping operations were started in 1962, the line was restored. The stripping operation, however, lasted but four years, and in October of 1975 the company, with words of finality, again filed for abandonment.[5]

In the early seventies Twila and Elmer Clark came back to Kempton, having bought Aubrey Bowers's house after Aubrey died. Elmer had worked in Cleveland for Continental Can for fifteen years but had always planned to return to Kempton. Twila was born in Henry, and for both of them the Upper Potomac Valley was home.

There are no signs of a Kempton renaissance. By and large the inhabitants seem to agree with one of Maxine Repetsky's daughters: "People prefer things the way they are." But since 1958 the Annual Kempton Reunion —the first Sunday in July—has drawn an enthusiastic crowd of several hundred former Kemptonites and descendants. In 1960 it attracted people from fifteen states excluding Maryland, West Virginia, and Virginia. The reunion is a great time to get together. It's usually held in a picnic ground, such as Island Creek Coal Company's park near Bayard, because there's not much space left in Kempton. The awarding of cash prizes of ten or twenty dollars is a highlight of the day. In 1977 the prize for the one who came the farthest went to a miner's daughter from Big Timber, Montana. A two-week-old granddaughter of a miner's widow got the prize for the youngest in attendance. Asa Lewis was supposed to get the prize for the oldest, but solemnly—and somewhat in the role of Kempton patriarch—he insisted it be given to Catherine Carbone, who had come from Bristol, Pennsylvania, with her son Tony.

Gladys Corbin, 1983.

Pete Corbin has passed away. Gladys and daughter Wanda now live in the superintendent's old house. Gladys's son has a mobile home on the next lot; it's the only noncompany house in Kempton. Children and grandchildren come to visit. The youngsters gather blackberries and wild apples on the hillside and play in the several-foot-deep pools of the Potomac just above the town. The aroma of peach cobbler and other good things still comes from the kitchens.

Across the beaver-dammed Potomac Valley, the long, low, green mountain is softened by a hint of mist. Isolated pillars, the sugar and red maples of flaming scarlet and orange are like notes for a Te Deum prelude to autumnal magnificence.

Year after year domestic and native plants have spread over the dirt streets, yards, and foundations of Kempton's hillside. As a result, the trees, shrubs, perennials, and herbs seem wildly oblivious to the laws of ecological succession. Untended in waste areas along the rusty railroad siding and Front Street and in moist spots near the river are Phoenician-purple ironweed flowers, five-to-six-foot joe-pye weeds bowing with heavy buff-pink heads, and asters, goldenrod, lavender thistle, and orange-hued impatiens splashing colors at random. Large older trees presently form a loose skirmish line along Front Street. Imperturbably, they hold back the tangled mass of wild apples, snowballs, locusts, berry brambles, arrowwood, crab apples, pines, mint, choke cherries, patches of periwinkle, maples, and honeysuckle. Dominant among the Front Street skirmishers are robust fifty-to-seventy-five-foot softwood trees—Chinese elms and poplars. Less successful is a line of white and Norway spruce that evidently suffers from some soil incompatibility. More vigorous is a recently planted row of red and white pines.

Scattered among the skirmisher trees along and below Front Street are nine Kempton company houses, their company-house pedigree still visible through the various lean-tos, extensions, and sidings added over the years. Most now have indoor plumbing. The roofs, without exception, bear television antennae.

In the clearing in the wild tangle above the town is Elmer Clark's pride: Kempton's 17,000-gallon water tank. Before the Clarks returned to Kempton, the town had been using water out of the mine shaft. It was frequently in short supply and sometimes had a bad taste. Everybody agreed something had to be done about it, so Elmer was volunteered to do it. It was a big job, but with help from both inside and outside Kempton, Elmer managed to get the tank tarred, build a cradle with railroad rails and cement blocks, and finally hoist the behemoth into place. Flow from a spring and flow from the tank, both by gravity, brought the water to the houses. Once he had it flowing, Elmer took a sample of the water to a laboratory in Davis, where it was tested and, though "not chlorinated," was declared the best in the county.

Martha "Twila" Clark, 1983.

Up the side of the hill behind the Clarks, Elmer has carried on his own private war against some of the plant horde that has taken over most of the town. Plot after plot of vegetable and flower beds is terraced along the slope behind the Clarks' house. Below the garden, in the middle of the lawn, a flagpole flying the red, white, and blue seems to underline Elmer's victory.

Not too long ago, Elmer redid Grace Dice's kitchen, and now he's busy replacing cast-iron water pipe with plastic (Maxine Repetsky's daughter helped him dig the trenches). Work is in his soul. He doubts that automa-

tion will take over from man, but if it should, he is convinced that people will simply die from lack of work. Like
ants who have had their nest destroyed, without pur-
poseful work they will die.[6]

WHERE THE POTOMAC BEGINS

10

Elk Garden: Big Vein Coal Town

...and one time the Davis Coal and Coke crew came through and painted the company houses red—all red.

—Interview with Roy Wiseman,
10 November 1976.

In the 1890s, before Kempton was even planned, Elk Garden peaked as a lusty West Virginia mining-farming community. Originally the town's site—about seven hundred feet above the river—was a salt lick and a handsome mountain pond, a place attractive to elk. Settlers came shortly after the Revolution. The region was one of prosperous farms.

A woodchuck receives credit for discovering the Big Vein. Coal from a hillside burrow was found in the groundhog's "diggins," and in time word of the find got to Henry G. Davis, who, with his brother, Colonel Tom, was searching for coal and timber after the Civil War. The Davis brothers rode up to John Nethken's farm by horseback, and, at the farmer's direction, two of Davis's men dug five feet into a hillside. Here they struck the Big Vein. Although John Nethken refused a lifetime railroad pass for himself and his family, he sold Henry Davis thirty-three and a half acres of "coal land" in 1871 for about forty-six dollars an acre.

In the late 1800s John had built a thirty-five-house village on Nethken Hill, and he rented each of the houses along with a farm plot for about twenty-five dollars a year. He also donated land for a new school and Methodist church to replace the log cabin that had served both purposes in the mountainside community for nearly a century. At one time, Nethkenville had a store, a blacksmith shop, and a community band.[1]

Meanwhile, a half mile away and several hundred feet below, Nethkenville's hillside prominence, Elk Garden, prospered and grew. Henry Davis had created a surge of activity with the opening of the first of his Big Vein mines in 1881. By 1885 three hundred Elk Garden miners were at work. Trams—narrow-gauge railroads—and inclined planes moved the high-quality steam coal to the West Virginia Central loading tipple in the Potomac Valley below.[2]

As the Davis rails pushed up the valley, ever-increasing loads of timber and coal from Elk Garden and other locations flowed back to Piedmont and Cumberland to be forwarded to western cities, eastern seaboard markets, and Atlantic ports. Mona Ridder points out in "Our Mountain Heritage" that the region's agriculture flourished along with the new mining enterprises:

> The farmers by no means suffered because of this new focus. Livestock and produce values increased considerably now that a convenient means of transportation to Pittsburgh and the eastern markets was available. The sale of the coal and timber from the farms enabled them to build larger houses and barns and sawmilling was a thriving enterprise in which to invest.[3]

West Virginia Central was vindicating the B & O's faith in the new spur railroad as a valuable freight-building partner.

But with the death of B & O president John Garrett in 1884, the close ties between the management of the two railroads weakened. At that time the B & O was the only means by which timber and coal from the Upper Potomac could reach Cumberland on its way to the marketplaces. To break its monopoly, Davis started construction of a parallel road, appropriately named the Piedmont and Cumberland. However, when the workers endeavored to lay tracks across leased ground of a cer-

Shay locomotive at Parsons Pulp & Lumber Co. near Dobbs, West Virginia, 1901.

Camp No. 6, Thompson Lumber Company, Davis, West Virginia, 1905.

tain Cookerly farm on the way to Cumberland, the B & O, working with the leaseholder, raised legal barriers. Davis obtained an injunction against the interference, and then B & O countered by dispatching legal counsel and over a hundred men to the scene. Arriving by rail from Cumberland, the marauders tore up the freshly laid Piedmont and Cumberland tracks and hauled them away to Martinsburg, West Virginia. Then they threw up a fence and, joined by miners from competing coal fields along George's Creek, established an occupying force. The sheriff arrested some of the invaders, but the court released them on habeas corpus.

While legal maneuvers continued throughout the spring and summer of '87, the Cookerly farm was the scene of mock warfare. There were miners and railroaders on both sides. The occupying force was well rationed and supplied; its size varied according to the threats of "troops" mustered by Henry Davis's supporters and workers. At one point a rolling mill-whistle called volunteers from all over Cumberland to board the B & O to Cookerly and to oppose a force said to be coming from Piedmont to re-lay the tracks. Surprisingly, despite the alarms and excursions, there was no serious violence.

The economic warfare had begun to pinch the miners

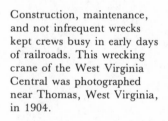

Construction, maintenance, and not infrequent wrecks kept crews busy in early days of railroads. This wrecking crane of the West Virginia Central was photographed near Thomas, West Virginia, in 1904.

in the Upper Potomac Valley since the B & O refused
to supply empty cars and carried Upper Potomac coal
only reluctantly. Finally, the matter began to draw to
a close when the court moved in favor of the Piedmont
and Cumberland Railroad. Then, at the same time, five
to six hundred Elk Garden miners arrived at the disputed
site, tore down the fence, and reopened the right-of-way.
The tracks were completed to Cumberland. If the B & O
had thought of further obstructionism, physical or legal,
the issue became moot: the new Davis railroad was carrying the United States mail—an inviolable cargo in
these near-frontier lands of Maryland and West Virginia.
The two railroads resumed good business relationships,
but the West Virginia Central was no longer in a position of dependency.[4]

Big Vein coal production continued to mount. West
Virginia Central extended a freight spur to Elk Garden
in 1888, outmoding the trams and inclined planes.
Passenger service running four times daily was intro-
duced in 1889, and with incorporation in January 1890
the town entered its biggest and burliest decade. The
Elk Garden News bragged that the growth showed what

Entrance, Big Vein Coal
Mine, Elk Garden, about
1919. Left to right: (First
name unknown) Droppleman,
Truman Wiseman, Jerry
Shillingburg.

a "railroad can do." Although the census numbered not more than six hundred people in the town itself, by 1900 there were about two thousand miners in the Elk Garden region. The fame of Elk Garden's Big Vein coal as a quality fuel for steam and domestic purposes was enhanced by the high acclaim accorded it at an exhibit of an amazing solid bed section, four feet square and fourteen feet thick, at the 1893 St. Louis World's Fair. The Maryland Bureau of Mines termed Big Vein coal an excellent blacksmithing coal and "one of the best steam coals in the world." Coal men called it a foolproof coal because even unskilled firemen could burn it with good results. The bureau further noted that Admiral Dewey's fleet had used it at the Battle of Manila Bay.[5]

The roof above Big Vein coal seams is known as "rashings," and because of its friable nature (its tendency to pulverize), "skillful timbering and workmanship of the highest order" was required of the miners. Davis Coal and Coke saw to it that its miners took part in the struggle against placing bituminous coal on the free list, with eight hundred Elk Garden miners petitioning the U.S. Senate in 1894. The petition "viewed with alarm" the removal of duty, which would enable Canadian coal to undersell American coal in its biggest market, the Atlantic seaboard.[6]

From time to time during the early 1900s, miners and railroaders of the Davis enterprises rendered other political assistance, sometimes out of personal loyalty to Senator Davis, sometimes out of perceived economic self-interest. But their support was not to be taken for granted. In the election of 1900, Elk Garden voters failed to follow his political guidance, thus distinguishing themselves from the people of Thomas, Davis, and Coketon, other towns with dominant Davis Company interest. H. G. Buxton, Henry Davis's nephew, wrote that the "rank" ingratitude of some Elk Garden citizens was deplorable.[7]

Davis Coal and Coke built about twenty-five company houses on some of the town land it owned along the tramway, and it leased other town lots for houses and business purposes. Elk Garden had a Buxton and Landstreet store. But more than a company town, Elk Garden had a robust vitality nurtured by a diverse economy. In addition to the several coal mines, there were other heavy enterprises: Isaac Oates's feed mill, three blacksmith shops, and a planing mill. Its villagers—like those in the Christmas window, busy at celebration and never-ending work—harnessed and released energy from the woodlot, farm, and mine. As if to capture this exuberance, the Davis painting crew came through one year "and painted the company houses red—all red."[8]

Elk Garden itself had two miles of two-inch-thick, six-foot-wide hardwood boardwalks and six hitching posts on Main Street. The *Elk Garden News* commented on the deplorable conditions in the town's alleys adjacent to hog pens and other places that gave off a "disagreeable stench." It noted that physicians recommend lime as an excellent disinfectant and urged citizens to keep the town clean.[9] In bad weather the town's streets also presented problems. One early spring storm left "a twenty-inch snow, and then slush, slush, and next mud, mud, mud."[10]

First oil, then gas, and finally electricity provided street lighting. The telephone system consisted of four lines of twenty-five boxes each, until C & P was connected to the Elk Garden phone system in 1917. A standard listing in the *Elk Garden News* served as a directory.

There were two horse-drawn taxis, a bicycle shop, and a livery stable. Davy Junkin's Delivery Service handled items at twenty-five cents per one hundred pounds. (Davy banked part of his earnings in his horse's name.) A chief of police, two constables, and two justices of the peace kept order. A most active citizen of the boom days was F. C. Rollman, painter, preacher, and undertaker, who also served as mayor and postmaster as well as justice of the peace. Four hotels gave lodging, and there were essential service shops: a gunsmith shop, a tin store, and a wallpaper and paint store. Mrs. Rollman operated a photograph studio over the post office, and there were also a jewelry store, a millinery store, a men's shop, and a tailor. One of the two barber shops also provided shoe repair.

In addition to Buxton and Landstreet, five general stores served Elk Garden along with several bake shops and a butcher. Among the restaurants was Cannos's, which served soup and the "best ice cream you ever tasted." Felix Cannos also had a confectionery, where

Elk Garden postoffice during World War I. F. C. Rollman, postmaster from 1901 to 1915, also served as mayor, justice of the peace, coroner, and undertaker. His wife's photography studio was on the second floor.

Starting in 1889, there were two passenger, two freight, and two mixed trains daily, except Sunday, during Elk Garden's heyday years.

108

his big yellow cat used to sleep in the candy case. And he was an excellent gardener. One of the few immigrant Italians in the town, Felix said that he had left Italy because "he'd cut the gut of a bigga man," and he had to "get out."

There was a choice of doctors and dentists. A man could get health care for himself for one dollar a month, for a whole family for two dollars. Doctors dispensed their own medicine. Two undertakers, including Mayor Rollman, served the town, and three cemeteries grew by the Methodist church on Nethken Hill. Although Elk Garden was strongly Methodist, there was also a Catholic church for a while, as well as a Church of the Brethren.

Two opera houses and three bands—one Scottish (a number of citizens were Scots), one black, and one white—provided entertainment. Knights of Pythias were active for a time and then died out, but the Odd Fellows, who showed movies in the Odd Fellows Hall, endured.

Fourth of July brought picnics, parades, baseball at the park, fireworks, and dancing at Oak Grove. Sometimes the West Virginia Central would run special trains to picnics in nearby towns. Both Ringling Brothers Circus and Buffalo Bill Cody's Wild West Show included Elk Garden on their circuits.[11]

Big Vein Coal Town

Flag Day, Elk Garden, 1918.

Displaced when his home in Shaw was submerged by the Bloomington Reservoir, Victor Kitzmiller moved six miles to Elk Garden, where he continues to barber. A history buff, Victor is surrounded by antique furniture, old photographs, and Indian artifacts.

Although the town was dry, enforcement of the prohibition laws was lax, and the trains brought beer and whiskey from Maryland. Pure rye whiskey was four dollars a gallon. The package included a glass and a corkscrew. The *Elk Garden News* in April 1891 observed:

> Quite a number of drunken men were seen on the streets last Saturday. Some free hand fighting was indulged in near the mines, by which some were laid off for thirty days. Beer and whisky. Drink; drank; drunk. What fools these mortals be.[12]

And then there were the cider dives, at least five when counted from time to time. A glass of cider went for five cents, and the patent medicine to go in it was fifteen cents. The patent medicines were Schneidelem Schnapps or Lightning Hot Drops—60 percent alcohol—a cure for rheumatism, diphtheria, and all aches and pains. Finch's establishment had a dance hall and general store as well as a cider dive, but Morran's was probably the biggest.[13] The scene was like a western movie when, in the middle of the night, some of the young farmers—"all cidered up"—rode their horses down the boardwalks and shot out the big glass light globes. After several of these forays,

110

one of these young bucks was arrested and fined twenty-five dollars. That put a stop to that.

But the most excitement was the Big Fire of 1927. It all started at "Stagger Inn," a vacant room in one of the restaurants that drunks rented to sober up in. One of the guests delivered a kick, and over went the stove. Someone rang the fire bell in front of the Town Hall, and everybody grabbed a bucket and ran. The flames consumed four or five buildings, including Buxton and Landstreet, but fortunately it was not a windy night and the fire brigade brought the fire in check. The town was saved—for a time.[14]

But times could be slow even in boom years. On a muggy summer afternoon the monotonous sounds of the barber's scissors and footsteps on the boardwalk induced sleepy boredom. One hoped that the barber's story might break the somnolence:

> An eager salesman, fresh in town, asks the quickest way to the Post Office. The canny, quick-thinking citizen sagely replies (as the Post Office is just one block away), with a thigh smacker: the quickest way to the Post Office is to run.

For each new customer, the barber repeated his big-laugh story—over and over. In vain, one hoped the barber would find a new one.[15]

An Elk Garden institution, Norman's store does general merchandising today as it did at the turn of the century.

Beginning at the turn of the century, the population slowly began to decline for several decades. Somewhat ominously, most of the houses in the Nethken Hill community had been dismantled before 1900. The Big Vein mining extended under the homes causing dangerous sink holes. Some of the public and private institutions disappeared. Western Maryland Railroad removed its Elk Garden run in 1929 as the economy worsened, and cracks appeared in the solidarity of the farming and mining community. A few buildings of the early days— Norman's store, Cannos's, Odd Fellows Hall—remained like beacons, while others, sagging and abandoned, were finally torn down for lumber. Increasing economic and social complexities intruded. No longer would a miner or farmer want to paint the town red, all red.[16]

11
An Awful Mine Horror

It was a strange picture. In the early morning the brawny mine workers went into the slope. Toward evening these men of strong arm and nerve about broke down as they tucked in a sheet the bodies of their fellow-workmen, placed them in dump cars and pushed the bodies through the mine for a distance of more than a mile to the main entrance.

—Oakland Republican,
27 April 1911[1]

Two catastrophes stand out in Elk Garden's early history: the Big Fire of 1927 and the 1911 explosion in Mine No. 20. No one was hurt in the Big Fire, but twenty three miners died in No. 20.

Known also as the Ott Mine after Superintendent Lee Ott, No. 20 was a drift mine. The slope followed the coal vein directly into the mountainside just a few hundred yards above the Potomac at Blaine on the Western Maryland main line. No. 20 was not a Big Vein mine. It worked the Lower Kittanning seam, which was only four and a half feet high and very irregular, with rolls, undulations, and clay veins.[2]

The district mine inspector gave No. 20 a favorable annual report in 1906: the roof was fairly good—well timbered and well looked after. The report noted, however, that No. 20's miners did ''shoot coal on the solid'' rather than making cuts over, beside, or under the spots where they placed the explosives.* A furnace produced fairly good ventilation in the mine, but on the report's recommendation Davis Coal and Coke installed a large fifteen-foot steam-powered fan.[3]

Four years later, the inspector's annual report cited the fact that Ott No. 20 gave off some explosive gas and was very dry. Blasting with black powder or dynamite in a dry, dusty mine was risky business, because material that ''blew out''—backfired into dusty mine rooms— could ignite explosions of tremendous force. To keep the dust down, management ordered that it be watered constantly and that exhaust steam from the big fan be directed into the intake airway. In addition and because of the explosion potential, both District Inspector W. B. Plaster and Davis Company permitted in No. 20 only those blasting agents with flameless characteristics.[4]

On April 19, 1911, just five days before the catastrophe, Plaster made his regular inspection and found the mine in ''excellent condition, except that quantities of dust were noticed.'' The miners were removing the dust, but Plaster told the foreman to have it moistened, too. William Arnold, who was sixteen when No. 20 exploded, recalls that ''coal dust was six inches deep along the mine train tracks.''[5]

Four days later, on Sunday evening, the fire boss turned off the mine fan; because of a slump in coal trade, he thought it likely that there would be no work the next day. As it turned out, the only workers called the next morning, April 24, were those needed for cleaning up and moistening down the dust. Instead of the usual hundred, a small crew of twenty-eight men went into the mine. Some of the men were a mile or more deep in the mountainside—probably under their homes.

Three men, who were working outside near the mine mouth at 8:30 A.M., were the first to know of the

---

*''Shooting coal on the solid'' means discharging an explosive in a coal or clay seam without making cuts in adjacent areas. If cuts are made they can absorb some of the force and minimize the amount of the blast that will explode or backfire into the mine chamber.

explosion. They heard a sound like wind rustling dead leaves. Their attention was drawn to the mine mouth. A cloud of thin, dark, gray dust moved slowly out of the mine and grew larger and thicker each instant. And then there was an earthshaking roar. The shock splintered the underground roof props outward for a square mile or more. Coal and slate from the roof collapsed in great slabs. Smoke and debris belched out of the mine mouth and snapped the trunk of a maple tree a undred feet away.

Alarm flew along both sides of the Potomac Valley. Hundreds began crowding at the smoking mouth of the mine. Men hurried from other nearby mines. Nine-year-old George Burdock was in the front yard when his father came running by. He wanted to go but his father said it was no place for children.[6]

A bleak and melancholy vigil after the explosion in Ott No. 20. Federal rescue workers from Wilkes Barre, Pennsylvania, and Davis Coal and Coke officials from Baltimore rushed to the scene by special trains.

Five of the twenty-eight, in a wet section near the mine mouth when the blast occurred, escaped unhurt. There was no sign of the others. While families and friends held a grief-stricken vigil at the mine mouth, the rescuers began to fight and struggle through debris and choking smoke and fumes. The company set up a telegraph post in the little mule feed shed fifty feet from the mine mouth. Eighteen-year-old Roy Wiseman, telegrapher for the Western Maryland Railroad at Elk Garden, was hired, and for two days and a night he provided communication with the outside world. One of the first telegraph messages was optimistic: "We have hopes of rescuing all or some of them alive."[7]

Early that Monday evening, about a mile down the main entry, they found Wilbur Shear's body. Burned and cut, he appeared to have been running when buried

THE REPUBLICAN.

VOLUME 35.   OAKLAND, MARYLAND, THURSDAY, APRIL 27, 1911.   NUMBER 7.

An Awful Mine Horror

NEAR KITZMILLER WHEN 23 MEN WERE KILLED BY EXPLOSION OF GAS

Bodies of All the Unfortunates Recovered, the Last One Yesterday Morning—Unrecognizable Masses

Twenty-three men were killed by an explosion in mine No. 20 of the Davis Coal and Coke Company, at Ott, near Kitzmiller, on the Western Maryland railway about 16 miles southeast of Oakland Monday morning at 8.30 o'clock. The men were: Leo Dempsey, Wm. Hetzel, Od. Hershberger, Wm. Buski, Thomas Yost, Charles Wilson, Jas. Dempsey, Harry Trainum, Wilbur Shears, John White, Wm. Pearson, G. White, Thomas Wilson, Hawthorn Patton, Frank Pugh, Wm. Pugh, Jr., Lester Wilson, Ray Wilson, John McWilson, James Brown, Seymour Runion, Oscar Pritchard, John Pritchard.

All are Americans except Buski. The body of Shears was taken out early Monday evening. It was easily identified.

About half the men were married with families. The rescuers worked at great risk. There were two large parties under the direction of Robert Grant, the superintendent of the mine. Practically all hope was abandoned at the start of reaching the men alive. The smoke in the mine was stifling and this greatly impeded the progress of the workers. Many headings were filled by falls of coal and the way to the place where the men were working was entirely closed. Superintendent Grant took his men through another slope and into a heading near the sealed rooms. Work is in progress making a crescent through the wall of coal toward the entombed men, nearly two miles back in the earth. The gas or vapor lingered heavily in the mine and the work was possible only at

short intervals and the strain on the rescuers was terrific. There were, however, willing relays and by a constant force of fresh men rapid progress was made. Late in the afternoon the rescuers had penetrated the mine about 4,000 feet and it was estimated at that time they still had that distance to go to reach the men. As the way progressed the work grew harder. There had been no sound from the inside. It was the general belief that the men, even if alive, could not be reached in time to save their lives.

It is not yet known whether the explosion came from dust or gas. It is uncommon for gas to gather in the mines of the upper Potomac region, which are a continuation of the mines of the Georges Creek region. The Ott mine is in the upper Potomac field near the headwaters of the river. It is a low vein mine, employing about one hundred men, but owing to the slump in the coal trade, only about one-fourth of the regular force went to work and they were engaged in cleaning up the mine.

The entrance to the mine is on top of the hill several hundred yards from the main line of the Western Maryland. The coal is dumped on cars on the main line, being carried to the tipple along the tracks. The mine is nearly two miles miles long and the heading runs back almost to the village of Elk Garden. The railway station for the mine is Blaine. Immediately after the explosion the whole country on both sides of the river was thrown into the greatest excitement and hundreds of men, women and children gathered about the mouth of the mine. Many were parents, brothers, sisters or wives of those entombed and great feeling was shown. Not a few were wringing their hands and crying aloud, while others more courageous set about planning the rescue. It was fortunate that the mine was not working full or there would have been few in the immediate neighborhood to help effect rescue. Words was telegraphed Thomas, W. Va., and two engines with rescue crews and appliances were rushed over the Western Maryland railway. The Ott mine is isolated from the other mines of the company and as a result the work of rescue was slow in getting started.

Charred and mutilated the bodies of the men were recovered by frantic fellow-workers, who dug their way into

the mine in their efforts to save the entombed men from death by suffocation, the last body being brought out yesterday at noon. The remains were those of John White.

It was a strange picture. In the early morning the brawny mine workers went into the slope. Toward evening these men of strong arm and nerve about broke down as they tucked in a sheet the bodies of their fellow-workmen, placed them in dump cars and pushed the bodies through the mine for a distance of more than a mile to the main entrance.

Elk Garden is located upon the crest of a mountain, while the mine runs about 300 feet below the plateau. The miners who were entombed lost their lives directly under their homes, for the slopes run in the middle of the mountains, it being necessary to climb nearly 500 feet to the openings.

During the work of rescue George May, one of the mine workers, was overcome while attempting to drag out one of the mine the body of one of the victims of the explosion. May was with a corps of seachers, including Herbert Hanbaugh, Jacob Gregory and W. B. Roberts, of the United States Bureau of Mines Rescue service, who with George F. Kallum, hurried to the scene of the disaster on a special train, arriving at Elk Garden at 6 o'clock Tuesday morning. May is in a critical condition, as his lungs are full of considerable monoxide poisoning.

William Willis another one of those who volunteered to search the mine for his fellow-workers entombed, was also overcome from the gaseous poisoning. Physicians worked over him for several hours to resuscitate him, but there is little hope of freeing his system of the poison.

The hero of the day was M. L. Garvey, superintendent of the Davis mine at Thomas, who rushed into the opening when he heard Willis about for help. Mr. Garvey was carried out unconscious, and P. S. Klein and H. P. Copeland, surgeons for the company, brought him back to consciousness. After he had revived he again went to the mine and directed a corps of workers searching for the bodies. He had been in the mine for many hours during the early part of the day, but at no time did he feel the effects of the poisonous gas until he attempted to rescue Willis.

Supt. J. W. Paul, of the Government Bureau of Mines, of Pittsburg, was overcome while he wore an oxygen helmet. He was revived at the mouth of the mine.

116

by a fall of slate. His comrades covered him with a sheet and rolled him to the temporary morgue, No. 20's blacksmith shop. Later, a carriage bore his remains to Elk Garden's Town Hall, where Lee Ott had ordered the women to wait out of the way of the rescuers. They almost fought with each other to see whether the shrouded body was a son, sweetheart, or husband.

Hope for other survivors began to fade, but the rescue teams of twenty or so pushed on; working and resting an hour at a time, they slogged through Monday night and Tuesday morning and into the afternoon. Federal Bureau of Mine workers came in by rail and joined the effort. When caved-in rocks and rubble blocked the way, the miners went in through another slope—a second entry into the mine—and made a crosscut through the easier-to-dig coal. Fumes overcame four of the rescuers, who had to be brought back to the mine mouth where company surgeons worked to revive them. After many hours in the mine, Martin L. Garvey, superintendent from the Davis mine at Thomas, collapsed as he rushed to help another rescuer. As soon as he was revived, he was back in the mine, working and directing the men. The *Baltimore Sun* named Garvey the "hero of the day."

They found John Pugh and his son, William, lying together at a curve. The father seemed to have struggled for life. The son held a dry battery tight in his hand. Although an official investigation was yet to be held, Lee Ott, speaking for Davis Coal and Coke, said that either the father or the son was responsible for the blast. One of the Pughs, Ott maintained, had used an overcharge of Monobel, one of the permitted explosives manufactured by DuPont, to dislodge a heavy clay vein. A slip or weak area in the clay had released the force of the explosion, and a blowout ignited the dust that arose.[8]

By midnight Tuesday the grimy, disheartened workers had brought out nineteen bodies, rolling them on mine cars for more than a mile. Mercifully the bodies were wrapped in sheets. Early Wednesday morning, while some miners dug graves in the Nethken Hill cemeteries, others returned to No. 20, determined to bring out the three who remained. Death embraced Elk Garden and it was particularly harsh and cruel. One by one, the bodies of friends and relatives were brought to the surface, some "unrecognizable masses" so charred and broken that they were taken directly to the church and cemetery. No veneers of mortuary art softened the shock.

The *Baltimore Sun* noted that these "men were of a high class of miners, coming from good families in this section and were among the leading citizens of their localities, the most of them being prominent in church and fraternal order circles."[9] Moreover, Elk Garden had a hardy monolithic social-economic system: "Elk Garden is a secluded spot. Everyone knows the other, families have lived there for generations and it is probably one of the most exclusive clans in the State."[10] A strong rural community had predated coal mining by a hundred years, and coal extraction had grafted remarkably well onto the agrarian system. Even as the Big Vein's output declined, other coal seams nurtured the dominant industry and way of life.

Those miners who died in Ott No. 20 were part of this homogeneous, close-knit culture. Only one was foreign-born, the Pole Bill Buskey. With an average age of thirty-one, the youngest two were eighteen and the oldest sixty-one. Thirteen were married and the families large. Of the married men who died, one had three hundred dollars of insurance and the rest had four hundred. Elk Garden's town council formed a relief committee for the widows and orphans. One widow had nine children; three widows had ten small ones among them. Altogether the explosion in No. 20 had made forty-five children fatherless.

At Elk Garden sons occasionally replaced their fathers in the mines. When Bill Arnold's father broke his leg, the superintendent came down and talked with his mother, and though Bill was only twelve they put him on in the mine as if he were sixteen. Some boys started in the mines doing half a turn with their fathers and grew up to be working partners. The Wilsons, the Pughs, the Dempseys, and the Pritchards—fathers and sons—had worked side by side and fallen together.[11] Lucky Bill Arnold worked in No. 20 the Saturday before Monday,

April 24, and recalls vividly that when they found the big Irishman, James Dempsey, "he was holding his boy's arm, trying to pull him along to safety" just before the fire billowed from the blast and turned the coal dust into a holocaust. Here in the mine between father and son were the closest ties in life and death.[12]

A rumor made the rounds: Davis Coal and Coke would be reprimanded for not moistening the coal dust. In reply, company officials told the *Baltimore Sun* that the mine had been in good condition, and that Inspector Plaster had just given the mine a "clean bill of health." From Charleston, West Virginia, Governor Glasscock telegraphed John Laing, the chief inspector at the scene, to "spare neither time, effort or money in ascertaining the cause." Laing set Thursday for a cornor's inquest. At the same time, with sixteen experts, he tried to examine the mine for the cause of the explosion, but fumes kept them out until Thursday morning.[13]

The *Baltimore Sun*, which carried two detailed accounts of the tragedy, editorialized in its Thursday edition that the catastrophe "should not have occurred." Pointing out that the cause had not been determined, the *Sun* raised questions: Was dust the cause, or had accumulated mine gas been responsible? The exhaust fan, it suggested, may have been running only two days out of the week. Whatever the cause, the accident could and should have been prevented. "Those who take their lives in their hands to delve into the bowels of the earth are entitled to every protection that the law can afford."[14]

Thursday afternoon, the day after they removed the last three bodies, Coroner F. C. Rollman summoned a jury of six. Chief Laing examined twelve witnesses, including inspectors, workers, and Superintendent Orestes Tibbets of Davis Coal and Coke's mines at Beryl. Tibbetts, who had led some of the rescuers, testified that the Davis Company was not derelict: the mine foreman had just completed an inspection before the blast, the men had cleaned up the mine the day before the explosion and it had been in good shape. Testimony also developed that an overcharge of Monobel, a permissible explosive, had been prepared to move a heavy clay vein. But the vein's hardness was not consistent, and a slip, a wedge-shaped fracture, developed. Then large rock blasted and a stream of fire ignited the dust.

After ten minutes deliberation Friday afternoon, the jury brought in a verdict: a blown-out charge had ignited the dust; Davis Coal and Coke was not to blame. The finding, however, was that it was not the Pughs but James Pritchard or his son Arthur who had fired the blast.[15]

The 1911 Annual Report of the West Virginia Bureau of Mines carried the official comments of Inspector Plaster and Chief Inspector Laing. Plaster noted that he had instructed management to moisten the dust five days before the explosion took place. He said further that he had not known the exhaust fan was idle, and since the mine at times liberated small amounts of gas, he had not consented to the fan's being turned off. As Plaster's report then summarized, since the mine was dry and dusty, and "solid shooting" was practiced at times because of the coal seam's peculiar structure, the regulation required that only permissible explosives be used in No. 20, and

> we were under the impression that this was being complied with to the letter. However, it developed during the investigation that black powder and dynamite as well was being used by a few of these miners.[16]

The question of guilt became an ambiguity in his report.

Chief Laing's detailed report asserted that there was no doubt in the minds of the inspectors who investigated the explosion "but that dust was the main factor." The five who escaped had been almost a mile from the explosion. The very wet condition from the watering had stopped the explosion before it reached them, and so they reached the surface in safety. He went on, however, to make a circumstantial implication: "[while] it would be unfair, perhaps, to say that black powder was used in the shot that caused the explosion, we have every reason to believe that it had been, as we found black powder in the mine. . . . My own convictions are, that if the hole referred to had been properly charged . . . and a permissible explosive used exclusively . . . the accident would not have happened.''

Chief Laing thus attributed the disaster to a violation of instructions by one man who, as a result, lost his own life and the lives of twenty-two others. To avoid such accidents in the future, Laing issued what, in view of the normal work pattern, seemed to be a stringent regulation: a prohibition of any kind of shooting in dusty, dry mines while the men were at work, and the blasting to be carried out by the shot firers only after all other men had left the mine. The chief said that he knew the regulation would be a hardship on the miners and would perhaps curtail production, but he was determined to execute it and put a stop to death and danger from unnecessary risk taking.[17]

The United States Bureau of Mines reported the accident in one of its information circulars. Although it quoted the state mine inspector's report that some black blasting powder was used in No. 20, it also stated that the workings were not sufficiently watered. The bureau further reported that the state department of mines had issued orders restricting the shooting in dry and dusty mines.[18]

And so, according to the carefully worded reports and evidence, it could have been Davis Coal and Coke, the Pritchards, or the Pughs who caused the disaster in Ott No. 20. It also could have been a combination of all three.

Davis Coal and Coke's *Employees' Magazine,* which covered Elk Garden as well as Kempton, carried the gospel of mine safety to the company coal towns. Six years after the explosion in No. 20, the magazine ran ''Adrift in America,'' an allegorical tale of safety, life, and morality, by Matilda Bennear, an Elk Garden citizen. An orphan tells the story and the gist of it is this:

> The boy's father died as the miners had ''risked too far'' without timbering. Soon thereafter the mother dies from pneumonia and heartbreak. A kindly minister then takes the youth in but moves away and leaves him [the author gives no explanations for the minister's depar-

ture]. The young man, nearly fifteen, "with a heart filled with ambition," is again alone.

A Mr. Muldoon, who is taking a drove of cattle to Chicago, hires the boy. He pays him appropriately when they reach the market, but leaves him in the big city, once again alone. Then our orphan falls in with young men who take his money while he is asleep. "I should not have told these strangers about money," he says to himself, "because so many people are worshipping the almighty dollar, instead of Almighty God."

Mr. Kindness, a policeman who also "was left very much adrift" when he was a boy, befriends the lad and takes him home for breakfast because, as the Good Book states, "Be mindful to entertain strangers; for thereby some have entertained angels unawares." The policeman's wife, mourning the loss of their son, readily adopts the orphan.

Finally, Kindness takes the boy to Mr. Goodman who plans to establish a coal mine in West Virginia. Wishing to institute safety in his mine, Mr. Goodman feels there is much to learn from accidents like the one that caused the death of the boy's father.

Mr. Goodman tells our orphan that he does not believe those who maintain that charity cannot be part of business. Business and charity, he says, can be worked together; all that is needed is a "starting."[19]

Thus, in "Adrift in America," where the ministerial and agricultural foster fathers do not endure, it is the businessman who emerges and points the way to success and security under moral guidance.

12
Anxious Change

*It is apparent that home ownership, family
and community ties, and common heritage
from the past have combined to make this town
a relatively stable social group. All life is a
process of adjustment, however, and the people
of Elk Garden are now faced with a situation
that has significant implications, many of
which are not yet appreciated by a majority of
the residents.*

—Ward F. Porter, Jr., West Virginia University,
Elk Garden, West Virginia:
A Reconnaissance Survey of a Problem Town,
June 1952[1]

By 1923 only 2 acres remained of the original 315 acres
of Big Vein Coal in Elk Garden. Production in less ac-
cessible veins of poorer quality, such as the Kittanning
in Ott No. 20, continued to decline. The town's population, 581 at the turn of the century, had dropped more
than 25 percent by 1920. By 1929 the decline in coal
freight brought an end to rail service.[2]

In June of '23, workmen were paving the Northwestern Turnpike when a local Country Life Conference at Mt. Storm, West Virginia, focused on the
social change anticipated from the shift in transportation to highways. The conferees feasted under the trees
on a sumptuous country banquet, and the three-day program featured singers from Elk Garden, an educator

from West Virginia University, and a Sunday morning service at the Methodist church. A 4-H Club girl spoke on the "Four Square Life." The Reverend Mr. Rapking of Buckhannon, West Virginia, urged that "churches, Sunday schools, and farm community spirit" continue to play key roles in holding young people on the farm, "while the great road projects...bring the ends of the earth into our midst." Communities, he said, would receive a "whirlwind of destruction or manifold blessing," according to their degree of preparation for the change.[3]

The new, hard-surfaced Northwestern Turnpike, U.S. Route 50, connected the region with Baltimore and Washington. Thanks to it, the smaller mines developed a brisk business shipping coal by trucks to these eastern markets. But Elk Garden's rich coal base continued to shrink through the twenties, the thirties, and the forties; neither farming, timber harvesting, nor mining could fill the need for jobs.[4]

With the beginning of the depression, labor unrest began to build and, in 1933, a major strike shut down all the mines in the region. Here, as in Kempton, the sagging economy was bringing hardship to the miners. In the Upper Potomac Valley, John L. Lewis, president of the United Mine Workers, helped focus attention on efforts to obtain union recognition. Led by organizers, as many as five hundred men marched on the Elk District mines, threatening closure if the operators did not accede to their demands. Mine owners and foreman were assaulted, and buildings and equipment were burned. The mines closed down, and in time, as in Kempton, the union was recognized.[5]

April 1950 was the nadir for Elk Garden, as it was for Kempton and other coal towns along the Upper Potomac Valley. The larger mines closed and more unemployment swept the area. Concerned by this immediate crisis, which culminated three decades of declining population and employment in southwest Mineral County, the West Virginia State Planning Board initiated a study of Elk Garden.[6] The survey found a relatively stable social group (three-quarters of the citizens owned their homes) but high unemployment. Of the employable families in August of 1950, 25 percent were without work. Of the able-bodied men working, many had been forced to take jobs other than in their favored occupation—coal mining—and the unemployed were characterized generally by the inability to seek jobs elsewhere. About half the townspeople were dependents, and 70 percent of the men and women over fifteen were married.

About fifty-five—or one-third of the town's houses— needed major repair; most of these were more than fifty years old. Nearly all the homes had electricity, radios, and washing machines, but few had running water, inside toilets, or central heating. A critical municipal problem, which the mayor and council were trying hard to solve, was the lack of central water and sewage systems. According to an unpublished West Virginia Health Department report, some of the drinking water was unsafe. A number of town wells had acidic water, and in the summer of 1950 some wells ran dry. Mining operations in the vicinity of the town were partly to blame.

Three combination stores and filling stations handled food, hardware, clothing, and drugs. A fourth store also had a lunch counter. Three taverns served the community, but there were no commercial recreational establishments, and the nearest theater was in Kitzmiller, three miles away.

The town no longer had a Catholic church, although there were congregations belonging to the Pentacostal, Church of God, and Methodist churches. A second Methodist church was located nearby at Nethken School. Although the Elk Garden region was not "over organized," the survey described the large number of organizations as "impressive." Knights of Pythias and Pythian sisters, Odd Fellows, Rebeccas, Boy and Girl Scouts, and PTA had strong memberships.

The survey held out some hope for an Elk Garden renewal:

> Recent developments in the international situation and the ensuing changes in our domestic economy may affect the situation considerably in the near future. The

125

expansion of industry and the mobilization of our
economy could create heavy demands for coal and so
the coal industry might revive locally.[7]

Still, the study's conclusion was not encouraging: coal
mining was on the decline and there was little prospect
of substantial forestry or agricultural enterprise to offset it. "The most likely and promising solution to Elk
Garden's problem" was "an increase in out-migration."[8]

Coal miner Jessie Reel had moved to Elk Garden during this period. Of Dutch-Irish background, he was born
in Nethken in 1929. One of seven brothers and one of
four to go into mining, Jessie liked coal mining; it was
hard work but enjoyable and he stayed in it for fourteen
years. Married in 1948, the Reels managed to buy a
house and lot in 1953 at a time when Elk Garden seemed
like a shanty town. They had to pinch pennies to get
by, and many times Jessie just walked by the meat
counter. His leg was mashed and the muscles cut in a
bad accident in 1956. He could scrape together just
enough money to stay off the job for a month.

But it was hereditary arthritis that forced Jessie to
retire in the late '50s. His veterans' benefits from a hitch
in the navy paid for gold-shot treatments, which helped.
He found that lying down hurt worse than standing.
Determined to keep going, he pushed himself to get out
and talk with townspeople and do a little work each day,
like patching the roof.[9]

As if to fulfill the prophesy of the State Planning Board
study, Elk Garden's out-migration continued. From 318
in 1950, the population dipped to 291 in 1970. In 1973,
after serving on the town council, Jessie Reel became
mayor for a two-year term. The new sewage system was
still in the planning stage. Although a new water system
was in place, it would run dry in the late summer and
fall. But the town paved its first road in Jessie Reel's
administration, and he received a handsome plaque for
his work as mayor.

Elk Garden's next elected mayor was unable to serve
(the duties took too much time), so the council persuaded
Mrs. James Droppleman to take the job. She became

the town's first woman mayor. A native of an old family of Cross, West Virginia, about ten miles from Elk Garden, Patricia Droppleman had studied nursing in Cumberland and today, in 1984, is still a nurse at Potomac Valley Hospital in Keyser. In addition to her professional nursing association and Red Cross activities, she is on the four-county Home Health Advisory Board. Her husband, Jim, a member of the Elk Garden Town Council, is a shift foreman at the Westvaco Paper Mill in Luke.[10]

Clyde Burdock, George Burdock's son and former Elk Garden schoolteacher, served as mayor in early 1984. Clyde built the Dropplemans' house, as over the last ten years he has for a number of other residents. Young couples are buying most of the new construction; some young marrieds have built their own homes. Work in deep and strip mining is on the upswing, but still, as is the case with Patricia and Jim Droppleman, Elk Garden residents are frequently employed in other communities—for example, at a glass plant in Keyser, a chicken-processing plant in Oakland, and a Bausch and Lomb plant in Mountain Lake Park. The census tally for 1980 was still exactly 291, showing no change in ten years.

Water problems continued for a while. Orange water sometimes ruined the clothes, and when the system ran dry, tank trucks hauled water all the way from Keyser. Finally by spring of 1981, a line constructed from Mt. Storm brought ample water of good quality. The mayor and council have also made progress in other areas. The town has a truck and snowplow and has expanded street lighting. As money becomes available, more street work is done. The town leaders are still working on a sewage system.

Active citizens like the Dropplemans and the Burdocks are concerned about civic apathy. There's not enough interest in good streets, in the town's appearance, or in its future. Few are concerned about the town government. As one leader said, the people just won't come out of their houses. But there's substantial enthusiasm for the school and its activities. Jim Droppleman is president and Patricia secretary of the Athletic Association; under their leadership, just about everyone follows the new high school football team.

Parallel to school activities are the youth meetings of the Assembly of God Church and the Boy Scouts of Troop 40. As the survey found in 1950, these organizations along with the Odd Fellows and the Rebeccas continue to be important to some of the townspeople. Particularly strong are the fire department and its ladies auxiliary. At the same time, institutions in other communities, such as the Lions Club at Kitzmiller and the Girl Scouts in Mt. Storm, draw membership from Elk Garden and carry loyalties and interest away from the town.

The fate of the town still turns on the future of coal. Patricia Droppleman sees the relaxation of sulfur standards and the general increase in coal consumption as omens of growth. Clyde Burdock may not be quite as optimistic; problems of town improvement and home construction are real ones and hard ones to deal with. He does see completed Bloomington Lake as a boom for tourism, and he is fairly confident that Ott No. 20 will be reopened.[11]

But there's a limit to the productive mining of a coal seam. Revised quality standards, new technologies, and increased demand will go only so far. Limitations on economical mining are in themselves variables, adding to the uncertainties. While economic security for Elk Garden will continue to be elusive, in some of the citizens the spirit of the clan survives with amazing hardiness.

PART THREE

Preservation, Reclamation, and Prospects

13
The Second Passage

We want economic prosperity to come in a way that enables us to handle it, to cope with it, and not to be overwhelmed by it.

— Tim Dugan, Garrett County
director of planning, in the
Baltimore Evening Sun,
9 August 1977.[1]

Now the diminutive Fairfax Stone is almost surrounded by heaps of slate and a great black moat of surface mine trenches. Down from the stone through the rural industrial landscape of the North Branch Valley, machines and buildings are scattered in seeming disarray; but it is an arrangement that a mining engineer would interpret in orderly terms of synclines, anticlines, and coal vein geology. On a quiet afternoon when the mines are idle, green and yellow bulldozers and mammoth red draglines stand in awkward posture along the slopes. In the mist of the valley, their buckets and blades seem as strange as the angular branches and exotic leaves of Coalmaker and associates.

The older houses of the valley—some weathered, cracked and repaired, some still in company town rows—contrast sharply with the new generation of mobile homes. Powder blue or mustard tan, each mobile home is neatly cut, shaped like a shoe box and gripped closely to the ground. Each has its nourishing egg sac, an oval silver tank. Close by are the omnipresent pickup trucks, most of them new and freshly painted in predominantly primary colors. Under the raised hood of one, the owner—two legs and half a torso—balances in symbiotic linkage with the engine.

Northeast of Kempton on Table Rock Road are the aboveground structures of the new Metikki Mine. Great silos, chimneys, mammoth sheds, and long sloping conveyors overwhelm the deserted landscape; their geometry mimics and dwarfs the farm buildings clustered in the foreground. The Metikki mine is a drift mine. It follows the same Upper Freeport seam of old No. 42 at Kempton, running back into the side of the Great Backbone and reaching a depth of 750 feet. Instead of electric trains, as in the working days of No. 42, Mettiki uses conveyors to haul the coal along the steep underground slopes.[2]

Just below the settlement ponds of the Buffalo Creek Mine at the town of Bayard, long lines of sooty black hopper cars and gondolas wait, some already loaded for Baltimore, others to be filled. Near the Bayard rail station several C & O locomotives stand motionless awaiting their next task. The interminable low rumbling purr of their diesels is appropriate to these sleeping Chessies. Now part of the CSX Corporation, they are the fifth dynasty of the rail companies that began with the West Virginia Central and Pittsburg RR. Successively, Henry Gassaway Davis's railroad merged into the Western Maryland, the Baltimore and Ohio, the Chesapeake and Ohio (Chessie), and the CSX Corporation, a holding company that includes both the Chessie and Seaboard Coast Line railroad systems. Against the fresh green of the Great Backbone Mountain rising serenely behind them, these behemoths are the archetypes of the machine in the garden.[3]

The people, the land, and the flora and fauna now bear passive witness to the unrestrained energy of those decades during which the machine—the railroad—brought the timber camps, the mining towns, and the descendant enterprises to open the frontier, welded the lands together, and put the "noble country alongside the sea."[4] This was the song of the first passage through the valley, when the noble country yielded the richness of its virgin forests and its fabulous wealth of coal:

> Singing my days,
> Singing the great achievements of the present,
> Singing the strong, light works of engineers....[5]

Today there are songs of a second passage. Now there are perceptions of formerly unappreciated values of the river and the land, perceptions awakened in the years of the environmental crusade of the 1960s and 1970s. The engineers of the development decades, who are seen as neither comprehending nor regulating development in harmony with the biosphere, are now popularly held in disdain. Still, despite the new awareness, plans for the future of the North Branch Valley seem fragmented. Understandably, for with their new knowledge planners have so many more new implications to consider, the second passage matches neither the railroad's singleness of purpose nor the thoroughness and efficiency with which it exploited the land.

The complexities, however, do not lessen the enthusiasm to restore, preserve, and develop the valley's resources. To salvage and maintain the valley's human story, a young archeologist and a young historian have been at work with a crusading vision that sees beyond the gob piles and the yellow boy streams. Funds from the Surface Mining Control and Reclamation Act (SMCRA) provide support for their work, and their enthusiasm is carried along by the zeal for conservation that spurred the act's passage. In 1980-81 the archeologist, tall, slender Bob Wall, and a Maryland geological survey team surveyed the Great Backbone, its lesser ridges, and the flood plain along the North Branch, as well as the Casselman and the Youghiogheny rivers to the north and west. Bob and his team used predictive models extrapolated from findings in similar regions to locate the most probable sites where Archaic, Paleo, and Woodland people had their camps, work places, and villages.

Every dig adds to cultural enrichment and to the total knowledge of early man. To carry out a survey, however, the archeologist must first negotiate with land owners—coal miners and farmers—for permission. There is always the concern that mining and all associated enterprises and jobs will be stopped dead by the discovery of an archeologic site. Times have been tough enough for decades in the plateau lands and coal region of western Maryland and West Virginia, with chronic unemployment sometimes up to 25 percent. As some say, it's hard for a businessman to justify keeping men from work while outsiders dig up pieces of pottery and Indian bones.[6]

For three days in August of 1980, Donna Ware, a capable historian-preservationist with the Maryland Historical Trust, visited Kempton at the head of a Coal Region Historic Sites survey team. The team members talked with Wanda Corbin and Maxine Repetsky. The sisters were congenial, and they supplied old pictures and

The original siding shows through the torn asphalt of this vacant Kempton company house. The few houses still occupied have been transfigured by the addition of new shingles, insulation, indoor plumbing, enclosed porches, and TV antennas.

told of the company coal town days. Except for the Corbin son's mobile home, all the company houses were more than fifty years of age and so were eligible to be included in the survey. Donna's team photographed and took notes on all of them.

Initially, Donna thought Kempton was a prospective candidate for the National Register as a historic district, but after thoughtful study she decided that not enough was left of the original community for it to qualify. Little was left of the mining structures and there were only a handful of company houses. Furthermore, Kempton's company-house pedigree had been lost through the additions of asphalt shingles, lean-to kitchens, enclosed porches, and indoor plumbing. Altogether Donna's team photographed and made preliminary notes on twelve hundred Maryland coal region buildings—homes, churches, schools, stores, coal tipples, and barns. Some owners were as outgoing as the two Corbin sisters, ready to give memorized accounts of the family geneology and to offer some home-preserved delicacies while they chatted on the front porch. Others were apprehensive and anxious, exhibiting fear of the feds, the tax assessor, the stranger.

For a number of the coal region residents, history is the accounting of people and their lives. They see little relevance in the vernacular architecture of barns, homes, or commercial structures of earlier days, for to them these are only of utilitarian value. As they see it, buildings with decorative features have the greatest value for preservation.[7]

The preservation values of naturalists have brought other dimensions to the second passage. In the Kempton Beaver Dam Bog, a wild, orchid-filled, wet land several miles northeast of Kempton surrounded by a great grove of northern spruce and hemlocks, Maryland's Nature Conservancy and the State Department of Natural Resources hope to save two hundred acres. These naturalists identify the Kempton Beaver Dam Bog as one of Maryland's significant natural areas, a legacy of boreal flora and fauna that was the common landscape before the retreat of the glaciers. Here are Canadian warblers, northern water thrushes, and hermit thrushes. It is the first recorded site in Maryland of the red-breasted nuthatch. The creeping snowberry and the dwarf rattlesnake plant (one of the orchids) are plentiful, and in July the round-leaved orchid blooms abundantly.[8]

The Kempton Bog has at least seventeen species of wildlife rare to Maryland. The loss of this habitat would be another step toward the depletion of these species and the reduction of the total stock of organisms upon which man depends for industry, food, recreation, and medicine. By the year 2000, with the present rate of habitat loss and increased pollution, the Council on Environmental Quality estimates that 15 to 20 percent of the global stock of life species—the great genetic pool—will be extinguished.

There are three other western Maryland post glacial age tracts that the Nature Conservancy and the Department of Natural Resources wish to preserve as ecological units. In reference to one of these, the Glades, George Fenwick, director of the State Natural Heritage office, told the *Baltimore Sun*, "[it] is a unique community... remarkable and unmatched in the state," which has less than eight hundred acres of peat bogs remaining.[9] In May 1983, Steve Hamblin, director of the conservancy, a young lawyer turned conservationist, was outbid by the Garrett Processing and Packaging Corporation for the Glades, in an auction at the Oakland Court House. The peat and coal of these unique biotic islands translate into jobs and fossil fuel energy and are clearly on value scales different from those of wildlife genetic pools.[10]

The *Oakland* (Maryland) *Republican* had favored ownership by the peat company but predicted that the conservancy would win the auction because of "its tremendous financial resources." This would remove more land from the tax base, which is a continuing concern of Garrett countians. Almost 17 percent of Garrett County is state owned, while in all of Maryland the average of state-owned land is a little over 5 percent. The *Republican* also predicted that state ownership could well halt public access and definitely stop hunting just when the state had proclaimed an overpopulation of deer.[11]

Garrett countian Melvin Brown, a retired botany professor recognized for his knowledge of western Maryland ecology, told the *Baltimore Sun* that in his judgment the Glades need not be preserved because several other boreal wildlife areas would have the same rare species. Although, as the *Sun* pointed out, Dr. Brown is one of the ten partners in Garrett Processing Corporation, his integrity as a professional is well established by his position as Nature Conservancy manager of another Garrett boreal area, the Finzel Bog. According to the *Sun*, one of the peat company's shareholders noted that the company had tried to arrange for the cooperative protection mining of the bog. "We are not villains in this episode," the shareholder said. "We are local people whose families have been here for generations and we care about this environment."[12] Obviously, the resolution of conflicting interests in the second passage turns on governmental processes, business and employment, as well as on considerations of culture and natural habitat.

But much of the second passage has to do with the need to remedy the damage from active and abandoned mines of the Upper Basin. For this there is a dedicated persistence; however, the efforts and the results seem uneven. Regulations now control all active mining, whether surface or deep. In the case of surface mining, the law requires that the companies digging from the shallow coal seams restore the land to usable contours and provide vegetation cover. Some surface mining is termed daylighting—that is, recovering coal pillars and walls from abandoned underground mines. In these shallow mines the earth has collapsed, subsided into the rooms and passages, and has aged the mountainsides with gaping pockmarks and wrinkles, just as the miners' faces have been aged during the decades of picking and shoveling beneath the earth. Daylighting can return the earth above to smooth youthful contours, rejuvenated for farming and forestry, and can actually improve the land. But reshuffling of the various layers of earth and rock in the overburden can develop potential pollution problems in water runoff, so careful engineering is needed.

Anthony Abar, director of Maryland's Bureau of Mines, implements programs that use funds authorized by the Mine Rehabilitation Act for the reclamation of abandoned deep and surface mines. Surface mines have left almost ninety miles of rough and ugly cliffs in the North Branch Valley. More than 4.5 percent of the watershed is scarred and subject to wind and water erosion. But of the six projects under way in Garrett and

Strip-mine operations close to the Fairfax Stone, 1983.

Allegany counties in 1983, only one was for the North Branch watershed, and it will only seal a bore hole of an abandoned deep mine on the south fork of Sand Run. Such a simple, modest cost project, estimated at sixteen thousand dollars, involves complex geologic structures and the unknown rooms, passages, and dimensions of a long-forgotten mine. Diversion of the drainage— sealing and plugging the bore hole—can lead to problems that make the project both difficult and more costly. The seal could blow out and send killing surges of acid water, or slugs, coursing downstream; or the seal could cause the water table to rise and contaminated overflow to seep into neighboring wells.[13]

When drainage from abandoned deep mines is polluted, sulfate- and iron-laden water oozes continuously. As a result, many of the streams in the North Branch watershed are now biological deserts. Laurel Run, which contributes one-third of the North Branch flow above the Bloomington Dam, has a hostile pH of 2.8. Because there is little life except for some acid-tolerant algae and insects, the water is usually crystal clear, but the rocks are stained with yellow boy. As the *Baltimore Evening Sun* observed in 1977, "it will be a long time before trout swim in the Laurel Run or mothers worry more about drownings than bleachings in the mountain streams."[14]

138

The active deep mines are prohibited from discharging acid waters. However, overtreatment of the minewater discharge—even to an alkaline pH 9 by some mine operators—can neutralize the acid to the benefit of a lifeless receiving stream. The pH of the Stony River, a West Virginia tributary that receives highly limed discharge, has risen steadily for several years. The West Virginia Wildlife Resources people hope to stock the stream with fingerlings, young fish no longer than a finger. The discharge from the Island Creek Coal Company's $7.5 million treatment plant at Bayard has raised the river's pH at that point to an excellent 6.7. After a fine largemouth bass population almost disappeared in the late '70s from Mt. Storm Lake at the head of the Stony River, the Vepco plant began again to overlime its discharge. Now the fish are coming back. Fishing in some spots is possible again in the North Branch and its tributaries. Neither the coal companies nor the utilities are adverse to the public relations value in overtreating discharge; they know the fishermen can be counted on to carry the good word.[15] Nevertheless, with different parts of the watershed receiving varying quantities and qualities of polluted and treated water as well as sediment, drawing a fishing map would be a pretty helter-skelter affair.

Tony Abar feels that he must devise a plan that first gives highest priority to safety and health considerations and then deals with the greatest quantity of the most acidic drainage. Part of the problem with which he and all mining engineers are confronted is the lack of good reliable technology to deal with abandoned deep mine drainage problems. As the acid-laden water continues to flow, researchers continue to search for economically effective solutions—techniques using detergents, inert gases, mine seals—to thwart the adverse iron and acid chemistry of the coal mines. As might be the case in dealing with the south fork of Sand Run, the cure can be worse than the disease.

Money to fund reclamation of abandoned mine sites will continue to be available from the tax on Maryland coal operators. Still, without significant breakthroughs in techniques to deal with the drainage and without treatment plants to deal with specific drainage sources, progress toward improving the streams of the North Branch watershed is likely to be slow.[16]

So the forecast for the quality of Bloomington Lake, chief recipient of the Upper Basin's chemical brew, has generally been less than good. A few years ago, one native of the area was fond of saying that the lake would be so full of poison that on being launched an aluminum boat would be dissolved before its owner could jump aboard.

A Mitre Corporation report, prepared for the corps of engineers in 1974, stated that lime treatment facilities to bring the lake to 6.5 pH would cost $1,490,000 with $260,000 required for annual operation. The study suggested that additional surveys might uncover more cost effective means of elevating the pH. However, the report also warned that a neutral pH, while improving the lake, could also lead to eutrophication problems if the heavy nutrient discharges from industrial and municipal sources, particularly at Luke, went uncontrolled. An earlier 1972 corp of engineers report said that the impoundment would place in temporary storage almost 95,000 acre-feet of water with a pH ranging from 2.7 to 4.9. This same study quoted Dr. R.B. Rozelle of Wilkes College, Pennsylvania, who reviewed the forecast on reservoir conditions. He stated that even partial acid abatement in the upstream areas could result in significant improvements in Bloomington Lake. Dr. Rozelle pointed out that where the pH of the North Branch waters reached 5.5, both iron and aluminum would tend to precipitate and better quality water would reach the impoundment. If the pH of the lake were to rise to 6.0 or better, a normal lake biota would begin to develop. But variations in flow and surges of low quality acid slugs are imponderables in such complex chemical-biological equations.

Nevertheless, by 1980 the pH in the new lake was 4.9. As the reservoir continued to fill, the pH rose, and by the spring of 1982, both at the lake bottom and surface, it hovered between 6.0 and 6.5. Sharp-eyed fishermen have since seen some bass, blue gill, and chub. Maryland and West Virginia wildlife departments reacted with enthusiasm to the lake's apparently growing potential for fishlife. Both agencies began releasing large numbers of fish into the river below the dam and into the lake itself: one-half-inch walleyes and fingerling rainbow trout in quantities of 1,200,000 and 18,000 respectively.

Russ Newman, superintendent for the Bloomington Dam and Lake, is certain that the heavy liming by upstream installations could well account for the lake's neutrality, but he is cautious about the future for both the released fish and anglers' luck. He is concerned about possible high biological oxygen demand in the lake as well as high levels of lime, iron, and sulfate. These chemicals can be inimical to the aquatic world. The best fish sought by anglers are those most sensitive to dissolved chemicals and organic matter.[17]

Low-level dams and weirs have always been common on the Potomac River, providing means for early settlers and Indians to catch fish and for canal operators to divert water into the Patowmack and C & O canals. But Bloomington Dam is the only high-level dam on the river's main stem to become a reality, and it exists not to provide the dreamed-of trans-Allegheny transportation route but for water quality, water storage, and flood control.

Actually, as late as the 1930s, leaders in commerce and government had still sought a transportation corridor through the Alleghenies to Pittsburgh. The corps of engineers proposed four possible inland navigation routes, and one of the plans was for a canal to ascend the Potomac North Branch to Gorman, Maryland, and, as George Washington proposed, push westward through the Great Backbone Mountain to the Youghiogheny in the Ohio-Mississippi watershed. This mammoth scheme would have provided a twelve-foot channel and twenty-seven dams in the Potomac, a two-mile tunnel under the mountain, and a bonus production of a billion kilowatts of prime energy.[18] But such an enterprise has no place in the schemes for the Potomac or Bloomington Dam today.

To fulfill Bloomington Dam's several missions, Russ Newman receives his instructions from Baltimore headquarters, which looks at diverse needs and resources of a large Middle Atlantic region. Water quality for better fishing downstream; water supply for the Washington metropolis; flood abatement, particularly for Luke and Piedmont; and recreation on the lake itself are all to be served. These various goals, however, cannot necessarily be served in harmony.

For the people of the Upper North Branch Valley, Bloomington Lake's recreation potential promises to strengthen the economies of Mineral County and the town of Elk Garden, communities that have been in decline since the early twentieth century. The corps has opened a picnic area and a ninety-site campground on the West Virginia side of the lake, only a few miles north of Elk Garden. Sailing and waterskiing are permitted. Swimming is not forbidden, but neither is it encouraged. Though the boat launch area is getting heavy usage, it may be restricted when downstream droughts take precedence and cause lake drawdowns.[19]

Those engaged in the river rafting business have made trial runs from the face of the Bloomington Dam to Luke. It is estimated that from four to eight hundred people a day could be attracted to rafting through this part of the old coal mine valley.[20] Even with its quality problems and the conflicting demands for its water, in a region of few recreational amenities Bloomington Lake is a significant asset. There will surely be more vacation cottages and second homes, as well as new commercial and even some industrial development. The lake could be a catalyst in revitalizing Elk Garden and the region.

In all of this the question of preparedness in community and government planning is paramount. With a dearth of community services and little governmental framework in place, rapid residential and industrial development could cause some problems in the future as troublesome as those found today. The 1974 Mitre Corporation report expanded on this question of preparedness to deal with what might be perceived as an influx of prosperity in the Elk Garden region:

The general level of social services within the Basin is considered to be marginally adequate. Any plan to improve water quality may increase socio/economic conditions to a point where these services are totally inadequate and the area would regress back to a status perhaps below current levels. Thus it is recommended that any plans for improvement of water quality be coordinated with plans for improving social services so that the area develops in a balanced fashion.[21]

The future for coal mining in the valley, tied as it is to worldwide considerations, can hardly be certain. There is, however, a substantial advocacy for coal, and a tacit faith that its one-time importance in the national economy will be renewed. In the summer of 1983 the county had only begun to come out of a recession, and the Metikki Mine was operating half time, with one shift of men working one week and another the next. Nevertheless, Metikki's chief engineer, Blucher Allison, was confident. "Coal," he said flatly, "is one of the mainstays of the world's energy economy."[22]

Respected national and international authorities agree with Allison. Coal has massive worldwide reserves, a fact of critical importance to energy planners contemplating another oil shortage. Barring unforeseen—even undreamed-of—radical breakthroughs in technology, coal will continue to be a vital source for world energy needs for at least several decades into the twenty-first century.

14

Beyond the Valley

If present trends continue, the world in 2000 will be more crowded, more polluted, less stable ecologically, and more vulnerable to disruption than the world we live in now. Serious stresses involving population, resources, and environment are clearly visible ahead. Despite great material output, the world's people will be poorer in many ways than they are today.

> —The Global 2000 Report to the President.
> Prepared by the Council on Environmental Quality,
> Department of State, 1980.[1]

Today's difficulties, serious as they are, are growing pains in a world half way through a great transition that will ultimately yield enormous benefits from the spread of progress and the greater control of technology for the good of all.

> —"Don't Expect Doomsday," Herman Kahn and
> Mitchell Ford,
> New York Times, 3 October 1980[2]

While coal is a cornerstone of the globe's energy storehouse, it is at the same time a major contributor to world environmental problems. In just several decades, the use of coal has released into the atmosphere prodigious quantities of sulfur and carbon that had been stored for eons by the photochemistry of the Permian and Carboniferous forests. As a result, coal is a major contributor to acid deposition—often referred to as acid rain—and to the atmospheric buildup of carbon dioxide, a component that could possibly cause atmospheric

heating through the so-called greenhouse effect. Leaders in the environmental field identify acid deposition and the atmospheric buildup of carbon dioxide as two of the world's three worst environmental time bombs, the third being toxic chemical buildup.[3]

Mist of a fall morning cloaks mine waste in North Branch Valley.

Academic journals and the popular press—sometimes with cover stories—chronicle acid deposition as the cause of severe degradation of the environment, citing as examples critical fish depletion and biological damage to tens of thousands of Scandinavian, Adirondack, and Canadian lakes; lead and copper contamination of Massachusetts and Swedish water supplies; massive timber damage to New England and East and West German forests; accumulated genetic effects reported by Soviet scientists; and ugly, irreparable damage to priceless historic structures, from the Cologne Cathedral and St. Paul's in London to the Royal Palace in Amsterdam and Trajan's Column in Rome. While there is evidence in some cases that acid rain has a beneficial fertilizing effect on crops, it is also reported to cause astronomical agricultural losses, up to $600 million a year in West Germany alone.[4]

145

The problem of acid deposition confronts politicians, biologists, government officials, miners, conservationists, consumers, power-plant operators, industrialists, foresters, and farmers. Their concerns drive vehement debates among international organizations, nations, and factions and regions within nations. All tend to agree on the seriousness of the problem and the need for more research. Beyond these two points, however, and especially on questions of responsibility and appropriate solutions, there is no consensus.

Because of the strong environmental movement in the United States, legislation requiring stricter control of acid-rain-producing pollutants may be passed within the next few years. Similar action may occur in a few other heavily impacted and technologically developed nations, such as West Germany and Sweden. However, it is unlikely that such action will affect an immediate major change in the course of environmental degradation by acid rain. Coal is a reasonably priced fuel available for large parts of the third world, and those developing nations that have large coal resources of high sulfur content will face increased acid deposition problems as their populations and industries grow. Chinese scientists, for example, already recognize this potential problem in the high sulfur coal of their southern provinces. But it is highly improbable that the third world nations, only now beginning their versions of the industrial revolution, can even begin to resolve the acid deposition questions. Overwhelmed as they are with mammoth problems of poverty and international debt, these countries are not inclined to assign high priority either to sulfur dioxide cleanup efforts or to fuel substitution programs. While some leaders speak of coping with the problem immediately, a familiar theme is resignation to the trade-off of development for some decades of polluted air.[5]

Even with agreement on the need for action and the type of technology needed to achieve success, problems rise to confound policy makers. The 1970 Clean Air Act set ambient air quality and emission standards for a variety of pollutants and sources. Industrial sources, especially utilities and smelters, tried to meet the air quality standards by constructing tall stacks that diluted and dispersed the pollution. The results were almost two hundred stacks over five hundred feet high and twenty over one thousand. It seems quite likely that the higher stacks have aggravated the problem and are responsible for acidic deposition at points hundreds, even thousands, of miles away.[6] In Sweden, a program to regenerate aquatic life in acidified lakes has involved lime aerosol spraying onto the water surface through huge pressurized hoses. Although the treatment has resulted in new stocks of fish being able to reproduce, the spraying destroys all the vegetation on the lakeshore. Exchanging lakeshore beauty for stocks of fish is a cruel trade-off in this Nordic country. Fishing is a national pastime in Sweden and involves more than one hundred thousand anglers.[7]

But even with side effects, it is possible to reverse some of the damage to the environment from acidic water, as has happened in parts of the North Branch of the Potomac. Streams and lakes can be rejuvenated; although the new ecosystems may differ from the originals when the character of the water is altered and the biotic community follows a different evolutionary path. Only time will tell, in some cases, whether a new plant and animal habitat has made a stream or lake more or less valuable to man. Where acid deposition has chemically altered forest soil so as to release aluminum and other metals toxic to tree roots, it could well take decades or several centuries for forests to recover from the damage.[8]

Probably a case can be made that acid deposition will not be an element fatal to man's ecosystem: even with poor, uneven remedies in some regions and none in others, the worst damage will be a severe degrading of the quality of life and health for some of the world's people. Nevertheless, acid deposition is not the first nor will it be the last distressing side effect of our well-intentioned use of technology. Other important chemicals that man has cycled in great quantities into his ecosystem, which for a time made a better world but which were later found to be extremely harmful, include DDT, PCB, and EDB.

Critical in the consideration of man's chemical alteration of the biosphere is the buildup of carbon dioxide.

Carbon dioxide, a constituent of the earth's atmosphere, produces the greenhouse effect. It allows the sun's radiation to pass through to the earth but prevents some of the infrared radiation (heat) from returning to space. If all other interacting components of the earth's climate system stayed the same, an increase in carbon dioxide would mean an increase in the earth's temperature. But there is no scientific agreement on the effects of important climate system variables, which could nullify or defer the atmospheric heating despite an increase in carbon dioxide. The absorptive capacity of the world's oceans for both heat and carbon dioxide and the reflective effect of possible increases in cloud cover are strongly debated unknowns.[9]

For the last forty years, atmospheric carbon dioxide has built up at a steady rate in proportion to the increased global use of fossil fuels. Dr. Melvin Calvin of the University of California at Berkeley stated the matter succinctly in testimony before a House of Representatives subcommittee: "The problem lies in the combustion of carbon that has been in the Earth for several million years, and we are burning it at a rate millions of times greater than it was laid down."[10]

Therefore, authorities can agree neither on how large the continuing buildup of carbon dioxide in the atmosphere will be over time nor on what the consequences will be for man and civilization. Some predict near doomsday—drastic, even catastrophic changes in the world's environment and civilization; others predict an almost latter-day Garden of Eden, with a greatly enhanced and stabilized agriculture and few adverse side effects.

Those scientists who decry the doomsayers point out that in the last ten years the global atmospheric temperatures have not risen in proportion to the increasing carbon dioxide levels. But this brings expressions of heightened concern that the heating trend is really being masked, possibly by ocean absorption of heat. Some warn that complacency and continued worldwide fossil fuel usage will produce a heating trend that will take centuries to reverse, with the reversal coming too late to offset the ill effects.[11]

And the results of this heating trend could indeed be ominous, according to concerned scientists and institutions like the Council on Environmental Quality, which sees the world continuing to burn fossil fuels into the twenty-first century. With a doubling of atmospheric carbon dioxide, the average global temperature will rise three degrees centigrade. The polar regions, however, could heat up as much as seven to ten degrees during the winter. Resulting expansion of upper ocean waters, and melting of continental ice from Greenland and Antarctica and of ice in high mountains could produce a rise in sea level approaching one meter over the next one hundred years. But if portions of the West Antarctic ice sheet were to collapse completely, the sea level could rise five to eight meters within several decades to several centuries. Just a five-meter rise would mean the gradual evacuation of 5 percent of the coastal population of the United States alone. The *Baltimore Sun* reported that if the Environmental Protection Agency's highest ocean rise scenario came true, Ocean City, Maryland, would become a medieval city, with a great sea wall on the Atlantic and high bulkheads on the bay side. The Chesapeake Bay would be radically altered, valuable marshes would be drowned, salt water would intrude into tributaries, and hazardous waste sites would be flooded, creating numerous problems of water supply and pollution.[12]

The concerned scientific community concedes some possible benefits from climatic change induced by carbon dioxide but points out that the agricultural industry in some regions would be nearly destroyed, bringing major refugee and hunger problems. Changes in rainfall patterns could turn great food-producing areas of the world into wastelands. Some rivers that supply irrigation waters would be dramatically reduced, while others would become flood prone.[13]

The optimists in the scientific community have a much different view. They see substantial biological benefits from a carbon dioxide doubling: lengthened growing seasons at medium and higher latitudes and increased productivity of rice, wheat, alfalfa, and soybeans. In particular, they point out that some crops would be better able to resist climatic stress. Maize, sugarcane, and sorghum, growing in higher concentrations of carbon dioxide, would lose less moisture and yield more produce. Sylvan Wittwer, director of the Agriculture Experiment Station at Michigan State University, believes that benefit from agricultural gains could be greater than all the predicted negative climatic effects.[14]

What emerges on review of the scientific studies is a "mass of uncertainty." While concerned scientists and institutions feel global action should start immediately to curtail fossil-fuel usage, all agree—doomsayers and Edenites alike, as on the question of acid deposition—that more study and research is essential. The World Meteorological Organization, the UN Environment Programme, and the International Council of Scientific Unions hope that a consensus on world action can be forged in 1985.[15]

By now it should be obvious that the role of coal in the world's future, as well as in Kempton, Elk Garden, and the misty Upper Potomac Valley, is like the intricacy of a great web, a web meshed into a marvelous swirling blue and white rondure. Technological changes, governmental action, and economic forces warp and skew the strands. The web's complexity grows with each new invention for the extraction and transportation of coal and each concomitant anti-pollution device, and it is increasingly tangled by the shifting tensions of new laws and regulations (which will undoubtedly be changed in turn by court action and sparring attorneys), by economic spasms on the international energy scene, and by the permutations of domestic conservation and resource policy.

The philosophers of an optimistic evolutionary scenario—that man will continue to flourish in a changing natural world as well as survive the adverse side effects of technological change—are moved either by empiricism or by a belief in a predestined role for man. These are ethical convictions, some of them rooted in the same religious ground as those that drove Henry Davis. These philosophers have faith that the human saga—the spiraling history of discovery, dazzling technological achievements, and cultural advancements—simply will not come to a tragic ending. In their view, man is the dominant species, and his demise, with another form of life taking his place, is unacceptable and intolerable. Indeed, they maintain that man's genius will lead mankind to a greater glory.

But those less optimistic warn that man must endeavor to understand and live in harmony with the universe. These prophets teach that time can run out. Technologies beget changes, changes beget problems to be corrected by more technologies, and each new technology has physical, environmental, and social impacts that, for better or for worse, interact immeasurably within a constantly expanding system. And unless man assumes his guardianship and gives guidance to the global environment, the ultimate scenario could result: an evolutionary swing that disposes of man as it disposed of Coalmaker and associates.[16]

Thus do philosophers and scientists confront the future from two camps, each camp armed with strong ideologies. Predictably, optimists and pessimists draw their disparate conclusions, often from the same facts, acknowledging the ambiguities in the conclusions they draw until they are left with no other choice but to advance their arguments from faith, nerve, and intuition.

For those of us who reject the case for doomsday, there is a certain comfort in history. This is not to say that because man has survived man will always survive. It is, however, to recognize that folly and wisdom flourish side by side, as do skepticism and faith, and that there is probably a better chance that man's wisdom will prevail then that his folly will do us in. Man's achievements to date are enough to bear this out. They should be enough to give us courage.

Nowhere are these achievements written more dramatically than in what might be called the saga of coal, for in man's historic relationship to coal can be seen man's relationship to the material world as a whole. Primitive man knew nothing, of course, about the process by which Coalmaker's photocells locked sunlight in chemical bondage, the sort of miracle that today is likely to evoke pantheism in even the most skeptical scientist.[17] Nevertheless, seeing coal for the first time, he must have responded with awe and wonder, sensing primeval powers at work in its creation. Centuries later, man's genius emerged with the Monongehela tribesman who put the creation itself to work, crafting cannel coal into pendants for protection, power, and beauty. Later, harnessing his genius to his visionary nature, modern man opened the wilderness—awakening "the slothful giant"—and extracted the ancient energy to make "a wonderful life" that would be "the marvel of the centuries."[18]

The miners of Elk Garden and Kempton may have been dubious participants in this wonderful life, struggling as they did against the adversities of life and death both above and below the ground. All the same, they left a legacy of fortitude that stands as enduring testimony to the communal spirit and to the ability of ordinary people to endure, adapt, and, if need be, move on. From that legacy we can draw a measure of hope.

Out of the muck and the mire
Sometimes a flower grows.

—HAROLD STRONG GULLIVER

Notes

1. Coalmaker and Associates

1. Walt Whitman, "Passage to India," in *Passage to India* (New York: Haskell House Publishers Ltd., 1969), p. 8.

2. Maryland v. West Virginia, 217 U.S. 1-47 (1910); Charles Morrison, *The Fairfax Line* (Parsons, W. Va.: McClain Printing Company, 1970), p. 11.

3. West Virginia, Geological and Economic Survey, *Coal and Coal Mining in West Virginia*, by James A. Barlow, Coal Geology Bulletin no. 2 (Morgantown, W. Va.: February 1974), p. 9; West Virginia, Geological Survey, "The Romance of Coal," by James D. Sisler, Mimeograph Series I, Bulletin no. 3 (Morgantown, W. Va.: 1 April 1931), p. 3.

4. A.C. Seward, *Plant Life through the Ages: A Geological and Botanical Retrospect* (London: Cambridge University Press, 1931), pp. 135, 184; Henry N. Andrews, Jr., *Studies in Paleobotany* (New York: John Wiley and Sons, Inc., 1961), pp. 218-228.

5. Henry N. Andrews, Jr., *Ancient Plants and the World They Lived In* (Ithaca, N.Y.: Comstock Publishing Co., 1947), pp. 59-64.

6. Andrews, *Studies in Paleobotany*, pp. 218-228.

7. Seward, p. 224.

8. Andrews, *Ancient Plants*, p. 73.

9. Ibid., pp. 81-82; Idem, *Studies in Paleobotany*, p. 276.

10. Seward, p. 186; Andrews, *Studies in Paleobotany*, p. 91 and *Ancient Plants*, p. 52.

11. Seward, p. 162; West Virginia, "Romance of Coal," p. 4.

2. First Man

1. Frank R. Corliss, Jr. "Folly Run Cairn No. 1, 18-Ga-54," *The West Virginia Archeologist* 16 (December 1963):2-3.

2. Robert D. Wall, archeologist, personal communication, January 1984; Maryland, Department of Natural Resources, Maryland Geological Survey, Division of Archeology, *An Archeological Study of the Western Maryland Coal Region: The Prehistoric Resources*, by Robert D. Wall

(Frostburg, Md.: Maryland Geological Survey, December 1981), pp. 123, 125-126.

.3. Ibid., pp. 8, 111, 130-132.

4. Ibid., pp. 132,134.

5. Maryland, Maryland Geological Survey, *Caves of Maryland*, by Richard Franz and Dennis Slifer, Educational Series no. 3 (1971), pp. 63-65; Maryland, "Archeology of Maryland Caves and Rock Shelters," by Tyler Bastian, in *Caves of Maryland*, p. 110; Martin H. Muma, "Maryland's Largest Shelter Cave," *Maryland: A Journal of Natural History* 14 (January 1944): 62-65; Frank R. Corliss, Jr. and Henry T. Wright III, "A Preliminary Analysis of Recent Excavations in the Upper Potomac Valley," *The Journal of the Archaeological Society of Maryland, Inc.* 3 (September 1967):145-152; Corliss, pp. 1-4.

6. Maryland, *Caves of Maryland*, p. 65.

7. Maryland, "Archeology of Maryland Caves," in *Caves of Maryland*, p. 110; Muma, pp. 62-65; Maryland, *An Archeological Study*, p. 125.

8. Corliss and Wright, p. 146; also see West Virginia, Geological and Economic Survey, *Introduction to West Virginia Archeology*, by Edward V. McMichael, Educational Series (Morgantown, W. Va., 1963).

9. William J. Mayer-Oakes, *Prehistory of the Upper Ohio Valley; An Introductory Archeological Study*, Anthropological Series no. 2, *Annals of Carnegie Museum* 34 (1955):38; Corliss and Wright, pp. 145-152; West Virginia, *West Virginia Archeology*, p. 49; U.S. Department of Interior, National Park Service, *The National Register of Historic Places—1976*, p. 319.

10. Corliss and Wright, pp. 145-152; West Virginia, *West Virginia Archeology*, p. 49; Department of Interior, *National Register*, p. 319.

11. *Encyclopaedia Britannica*, 15th ed., s.v. "Southwest American Indians," by Laura Thompson; George H. Pepper, "Ceremonial Objects and Ornaments from Pueblo Bonito, New Mexico," *American Anthropologist*, n.s., 7 (April-June 1905): 190-194; Smithsonian Institution, Bureau of American Ethnology, "Two Summers, Work in Pueblo Ruins," by Jesse Walter Fewkes, *22d Annual Report of the Bureau of American Ethnology* (Washington: U.S. Government Printing Office, 1904), pp. 87-88.

12. Corliss and Wright, pp. 145-152; Department of Interior, *National Register*.

13. Corliss, pp. 1-4.

14. Ibid., p. 2.

15. Ibid., pp. 1-4; "State's Bridge Plans Revised to Save Site," *Baltimore Sun*, 15 November 1983, sec. B.; Robert D. Wall, "Excavations at the Cresaptown Site in the Upper Potomac Valley" (Paper presented at the fall meeting of the Potomac River Basin Consortium, Frostburg, Md., October 1983).

16. Pennsylvania, The Pennsylvania Historical and Museum Commission, *Indian Paths of Pennsylvania*, by Paul A.W. Wallace (Harrisburg: The Pennsylvania Historical and Museum Commission, 1965), p. 180; Charles H. Ambler, *West Virginia—The Mountain State* (New York: Prentice-Hall Inc., 1940), pp. 1, 33; James Veech, *The Monongahela of Old; or, Historical Sketches of South-Western Pennsylvania to the Year 1800* (Pittsburgh: By the Author, 1858-1892), pp. 34-35.

17. Archer Butler Hulbert, *Paths of the Mound-Building Indians and Great Game Animals*, vol. 1 of *Historic Highways of America* (New York: AMS Press, 1971), p. 137.

18. George Washington, Diary of September 1784, in *Washington and the West: Being George Washington's Diary of September, 1784. Kept during his journey into the Ohio Basin in the interest of a commercial union between the Great Lakes and the Potomac River—And a commentary upon the same by Archer Butler Hulbert*, by Archer Butler Hulbert (New York: The Century Co., 1905), p. 67; Charles Carpenter, "West Virginia Buffalo Trails," *The West Virginia Review* 8 (July 1931):333; "Extinct Animals of Garrett County," *Glades Star* 2 (31 March 1952):139-140. See also Frank Gilbert Roe, *The North American Buffalo: A Critical Study of the Species in its Wild State,* 2nd ed. (Toronto and Buffalo: University of Toronto Press, 1970), pp. 119-153.

3. Unlocking the North Branch Valley

1. Washington, Diary of 1784, in Hulbert, *Washington and the West,* pp. 28-29.

2. "A Traveler over McCullough's Path," *Glades Star* 1 (30 September 1948):299; "Pioneer Path," *Glades Star* 5 (March 1978):68-69; Charles E. Hoye, "Garrett County History of Pioneer Families: CVI. The Bruce Family," *Oakland* (Maryland) *Mountain Democrat,* n.d.; Washington, Diary of 1784, in Hulbert, *Washington and the West*; Archer Butler Hulbert, *Pioneer Roads and Experiences of Travelers* (II), vol. 12 of *Historic Highways of America* (New York: AMS Press, 1971), pp. 24-29.

3. *Oxford Dictionary of the Christian Church*, 2nd ed., s.v. "Tunkers"; *Westminster Dictionary of Church History*, 1971 ed., s.v. "Brethren (Dunkers)."

4. "First Settlers of the Glades Country," *Glades Star* 1 (2 July 1941):9, 11, 13; Maryland, Department of Economic and Community Development, *Maryland Historical Atlas* (Washington: Raymond, Parish, Pine and Plavnick, 1973), p. 11; Hulbert, *Pioneer Roads*, p. 26.

5. Thomas Lewis, Journal, quoted in Horace P. Hobbs, Jr., *Pioneers of the Potowmack* (Ann Arbor, Mich.: University Microfilms, Inc., 1964), p. 134.

6. Hobbs, p. 127; Morrison, pp. 5-15; "The Fairfax Stone," *Glades Star* 2 (March 1958):435-439; Maryland v. West Virginia, 217 U.S. 1-47 (1910).

7. "Fairfax Stone," p. 437.

8. Stephen Schlossnagle and the Garrett County Bicentennial Committee, *Garrett County: A History of Maryland's Tableland* (Parsons, W. Va.: McClain Printing Company, 1978), pp. 120-121; W. E. Brooks, *The Northwest Turnpike and West Virginia*, a Newcomen Address published under the auspices of the American Branch of the Newcomen Society (Princeton, N.J.: Princeton University Press, 1943), p. 14; Washington, Diary of 1784, in Hulbert, *Washington and the West,* pp. 27,37; Hulbert, *Washington and the West*, pp. 20-21.

9. Washington, Diary of 1784, in Hulbert, *Washington and the West,* pp. 9-13.

10. Ibid., p. 29.

11. Ibid., pp. 28-32, 70-77.

12. Hulbert, *Washington and the West*, pp. 134-138.

13. Hulbert, *Pioneer Roads*, pp. 16-17, 20-24; Washington, Diary of 1784,

in Hulbert, *Washington and the West,* pp. 58-84.

14. Hulbert, *Washington and the West*, pp. 180-187.

15. House Committee on Roads and Canals, *Chesapeake and Ohio Canal*, 19th Cong., 1st sess., 22 May 1826, H. Rept. 228; Frederick Gutheim, *The Potomac* (New York: Holt, Rinehart and Winston, 1974), pp. 252-256.

16. Charles M. Pepper, *The Life and Times of Henry Gassaway Davis* (New York: The Century Company, 1920), p. 10; Gutheim, pp. 260-264.

17. Hulbert, *Pioneer Roads*, pp. 30-37, 40-41; W.E. Brooks, p. 21; James Morton Callahan, *Semi-Centennial History of West Virginia* (Morgantown, W. Va.: Semi-Centennial Commission of West Virginia, 1913), pp. 106-109.

18. See the following articles in *Glades Star* 2 (30 June 1953): "Gorman—1928," pp. 193-196; D. W. Idleman, "Gormania," pp. 197-198; and "The Schaeffers," pp. 201. See also John Randolph Schaeffer, *Over the Alleghenies by the Northwest Turnpike—Now the Great Scenic Federal Highway* (Gormania, W. Va.: n.p., 1928), pp. 63-64; and Ambler, *West Virginia—The Mountain State,* p. 256.

19. Hulbert, *Washington and the West*, pp. 194-195.

20. Philip Pendleton Kennedy [The Clerke of Oxenforde], *The Blackwater Chronicle* (New York: Redfield, 1853).

21. Ibid., pp. 7-8.

22. Ibid., p. 54.

23. Ibid., pp. 22, 56, 64.

24. Ibid., pp. 218-219.

25. Ibid., p. 212.

26. Ibid., p. 213.

27. Ibid.

4. Making the Way Straight

1. Pepper, *Life of Davis*, title page.

2. Ibid., pp. 12-16.

3. Ibid., pp. 215-216, 279-280, 285, 290.

4. Ibid., pp. 19-21.

5. Ibid., pp. 24-28; Callahan, *Semi-Centennial History of West Virginia*, p. 61.

6. Phil Conley, *History of the West Virginia Coal Industry* (Charleston, W. Va.: Education Foundation, Inc., 1960), pp. 177-178.

7. John Alexander Williams, "Davis and Elkins of West Virginia" (Ph.D. dissertation, Yale University, 1967), p. 19.

8. Pepper, *Life of Davis*, p. 91.

9. Schlossnagle, p. 246.

10. Ibid.; Pepper, *Life of Davis*, p. 91.

11. "Davis Journal," *Glades Star* 2 (31 December 1951):125; "Deer Park Hotel," *Glades Star* 2 (31 December 1951):123; Williams, "Davis and Elkins," p. 93.

12. Pepper, *Life of Davis*, pp. 158-164.

13. Ibid., pp. 38, 287.

14. Williams, "Davis and Elkins," p. 98; Editorial, *Cumberland Times*, 27 October 1884.

15. Henry G. Davis, "National and State Politics" (Speech delivered at Mineral County Convention, Mineral County, W. Va., 15 August 1874), p. 24.

16. Williams, "Davis and Elkins," pp. 129-130.

17. West Virginia Central and Pittsburg Railway Company, *First Report, January 1st, 1882* (Washington: R.O. Polkinhorn, Printer, 1882), p. 1.

18. Pepper, *Life of Davis*, pp. 99-102

19. Ibid., p. 228; Idleman, "Gormania," p. 197; West Virginia Central and Pittsburg Railway Company, *Second Annual Report, January 8, 1884* (Baltimore: Wm. J.C. Dulany and Co., 1884), pp. 2-4.

20. West Virginia Central and Pittsburg Railway Company, *Fourth Annual Report, January 26, 1886* (Baltimore: American Steam Job Press, 1886), pp. 5-7.

21. West Virginia Central and Pittsburg Railway Company, *Seventh Annual Report, January 22, 1889* (Baltimore: Wm. J.C. Dulany and Co., 1889), pp. 8-9; Pepper, *Life of Davis*, p. 320.

22. Williams, "Davis and Elkins," pp. 23-24; Pepper, *Life of Davis*, pp. 97-98.

23. H. Paul Santmire, *Brother Earth* (New York: Thomas Nelson, Inc., 1970), pp. 28-35.

24. West Virginia Central, *First Report*, p. 5.

25. West Virginia Central, *Second Report*, p. 6.

26. See Roy B. Clarkson, *Tumult on the Mountains: Lumbering in West Virginia—1770-1920* (Parsons, W. Va.: McClain Printing Company, 1964).

27. Ralph Daniel Ranger, *Pacific Coast Shay: Strong Man of the Woods* (San Marino, Calif.: Golden West Books, 1964), p. 7.

28. Maryland, Maryland Geological Survey, *Maryland Geological Survey: Garrett County* (Baltimore: The Johns Hopkins University Press, 1902), pp. 280, 320.

29. West Virginia Central, *Seventh Report*, p. 7.

30. West Virginia Central and Pittsburgh Railway Company, *West Virginia Central and Pittsburgh Railway* (Cumberland, Md.: The Independent Job Room, 1899).

31. West Virginia Central, *Seventh Report*, p. 7.

32. Maryland, Maryland Geological Survey, *Report on the Coals of Maryland* (Baltimore: The Johns Hopkins University Press, 1905), pp. 534-540.

33. Marshall B. Davidson, ed., *Notable American Houses* (New York: American Heritage Publishing Co., Inc., 1971), pp. 238-239; John A. Kouwenhoven, *Made in America* (Garden City, N.Y.: Doubleday and Company, Inc., 1948), pp. 60-85.

5. Pride and Patriotism

1. Reprinted in "Kempton Makes a Splendid Show," *Our Own People*, Davis Coal and Coke Company, Cumberland, Md., August 1918, pp. 38-39.

2. James Morton Callahan, *History of West Virginia* (Chicago and New York: American Historical Society, Inc., 1923), p. 478; Pepper, *Life*

of Davis, p. 186; Felix G. Robinson, "Davis, West Virginia: Village of Undying Hope," *Tableland Trails* 1 (Spring 1953):37; Harold Williams, *The Western Maryland Railway Story* (Baltimore: Western Maryland Railway Company, 1952), pp. 91-97.

3. "New Mine Opened in Garrett County," *Oakland* (Maryland) *Republican,* 23 July 1914; "Awards Contract to Open New Mine," *Oakland* (Maryland) *Republican,* 24 July 1913; Garrett County (Maryland) Board of School Commissioners, Minutes of Meetings, 1873-1916, meeting 2 March 1915, p. 529 (Handwritten); Maryland, Maryland Geological Survey, *Maryland Geological Survey,* vol. II (Baltimore: The Johns Hopkins University Press, 1922), pp. 159-160, 251-252; Maryland, *Annual Report of the Mine Inspector for Allegany and Garrett Counties, Maryland,* 1 May 1914 to 1 May 1915, pp. 27-28.

4. Katherine A. Harvey, *The Best Dressed Miners: Life and Labor in the Maryland Coal Region, 1835-1910* (Ithaca: Cornell University Press, 1969), pp. 24, 70, 101-105.

5. Nina K. Duling, "Kempton: Memories of Kempton," *Parsons* (West Virginia) *Advocate,* 27 April 1950; Maryland, *Report on Coals*, p. 559.

6. Interview with Roy Gibbs (retired mine employee), Kempton, Maryland, 21 October 1976.

7. Interviews with Edna Lewis (widow of former principal, Kempton School), Kempton, Maryland, 11 November 1976, 21 November 1977, 8 March 1980; Interview with Ida Geroski (miner's widow), Kempton, Maryland, 20 November 1977.

8. Interviews with Gladys Corbin (miner's widow), Kempton, Maryland, 21 October 1976, 3 November 1976, 7 March 1980.

9. Duling, p. 6; Interviews with Gladys Corbin.

10. Conley, p. 201.

11. Interviews with Gladys Corbin; "Kempton," *Our Own People,* December 1918, p. 26.

12. "The Garden Contest," *Our Own People,* November 1918, p. 5.

13. "Kempton," *Our Own People,* February 1918.

14. "Kempton," *Our Own People,* August 1918, p. 37; September 1918, pp. 39-40; October 1918, pp. 32-33; May 1919, p. 26; June 1919, p. 18; November 1919, p. 3; December 1919, p. 25; "Third Annual Davis Coal and Coke Company Employees' First Aid Meet at Thomas, W. Va.," *Our Own People,* July 1919, p. 7; "Thomas—Coketon, W. Va.," *Our Own People,* p. 14; Interviews with Maxine Corbin Repetsky (miner's widow and lifelong resident of Kempton), Kempton, Maryland, 15 October 1977, 7 March 1980, 21 February 1983, 23 March 1983, 8 March 1984.

15. "Kempton," *Employees' Magazine,* Davis Coal and Coke Company, Cumberland, Md., 2 July 1917, pp. 34-36.

16. "Private Robert A. Quigley. An Interesting Speaker," *Our Own People,* November 1918, p. 1; "Our Service Flag," *Our Own People,* July 1919, pp. 4-5.

17. "Kempton," *Our Own People,* August 1918, p. 38; September 1918, p. 39; January 1919, p. 24.

18. "Kempton," *Our Own People,* December 1919, pp. 25-26.

19. "The Flu Epidemic," *Our Own People,* December 1918, p. 14; "The Influenza Epidemic," *Our Own People,* January 1919, p. 4; Paul T. Calderwood, "Community Schools of Garrett County," *Glades Star*

4 (March 1977):747; Interviews with Gladys Corbin.

20. "Explosion Kills Fifteen Miners at Kempton," *Oakland* (Maryland) *Republican,* 2 March 1916; "Kempton Explosion," *Parsons* (West Virginia) *Advocate,* 2 March 1916; "Fifteen Killed in Coal Mine," *Baltimore Sun,* 1 March 1916; Maryland, *Annual Report of the Mining Inspector,* from 1 May 1915 to 1 May 1917, pp. 26-29.

21. L. J. Lanich, "First Aid to the Injured," *Employees' Magazine,* 2 November 1917, p. 16; "Accidents by Nationality in Pennsylvania and West Virginia," *Our Own People,* November 1919, p. 13.

22. "Code of Honorable Names," *Our Own People*, April 1919, p. 8; Interview with Ida Geroski.

23. Lanich, "First Aid," p. 16.

6. Prosperity and Problems

1. "Kempton," *Oakland* (Maryland) *Republican*, 10 April 1924.

2. Ibid., 16 February 1922.

3. Interview with Anne Povish Schoen (attended Kempton Elementary School), Kempton, Maryland, 13 September 1977; Interview with Ida Geroski.

4. *Oakland* (Maryland) *Republican*, 3, 10 April 1924.

5. "Kempton," *Oakland* (Maryland) *Republican*, 10 April 1924.

6. "Foreign Born Kempton Miners Caught in Raid," *Oakland* (Maryland) *Republican*, 28 August 1924; Interviews with Elmer Clark (retired miner), Kempton, Maryland, 11 June 1977, 27 August 1977, 15 October 1977, 21 October 1977, 25 July 1978.

7. "Kempton," *Oakland* (Maryland) *Republican*, 6, 13 March, 10 April 1924.

8. Interview with Frank Anthony (Tony) Carbone (former miner), Kempton, Maryland, 3 July 1977.

9. Interviews with Mr. and Mrs. Edward E. Sollars (former Kempton miner, son of company doctor, and his wife), Kempton, Maryland, 5 January 1978, 16 June 1978; "Kempton," *Oakland* (Maryland) *Republican,* 13 November, 11 December 1930; Interview with Kyle Bennett (son of former Kempton miner), Kempton, Maryland, 7 March 1980; Interview with Ida Geroski; Frances Comp, "Doctors of Deer Park," *Glades Star* 2 (30 September 1951): 109-110.

10. Asa Lewis, "Asa Lewis, 1887-1977," *Glades Star* 5 (March 1978):61-63. This autobiographical essay was found by Edna Lewis following her husband's death; Interviews with Edna Lewis; Interview with Asa Lewis (former principal of Kempton School), Kempton, Maryland, 11 November 1976.

11. Interviews with Elmer Clark; Interviews with Martha ("Twila") Clark (miner's widow), Kempton, Maryland, 7 March 1980, 5 March 1984, 10 March 1984.

12. Lewis, "Asa Lewis," p. 62; Interviews with Edna and Asa Lewis; Interviews with Martha and Elmer Clark.

13. Glen Lawhon Parker, *The Coal Industry* (Washington: American Council on Public Affairs, 1940), p. 57; Interviews with Elmer Clark.

7. The 1930s—Tough Times and Political Strife

1. Interview with Tony Carbone.

2. Interviews with Stanley Turek (Kempton miner and union president), Kempton, Maryland, 2 July 1978, 13 July 1978, 19 March 1979; Interview with Ralph Calandralla (physician), Kitzmiller, Maryland, 12 November 1976; Maryland, Bureau of Mines, *Tenth Annual Report*, Calendar Year 1932, p. 57.

3. Interviews with Gladys Corbin; Interviews with Stanley Turek; Interviews with Edna and Asa Lewis; Interviews with Maxine Repetsky.

4. Davis Coal and Coke Company, *Davis Coal News*, Baltimore, Maryland, January 1933, p. 3.

5. Ibid., August 1935, p. 3.

6. Ibid., September 1934, p. 3.

7. Ibid., June 1933, p. 9.

8. *Oakland* (Maryland) *Republican*, 17 November 1932; 12 November 1936; 16 November 1944.

9. Interviews with Edna Lewis; Interviews with Gladys Corbin; Interviews with Elmer Clark.

10. Interviews with Stanley Turek; Interviews with Gladys Corbin.

11. Kempton (Maryland) Homemakers Club, Minutes of Monthly Meetings, 1938-1943 (Handwritten); Kempton (Maryland) Women's Society of Christian Service in the Local Church, Minutes of Monthly Meetings, 1943-1944 (Handwritten); Kempton (Maryland) Ladies Aid Society, Minutes of Monthly Meetings, 1933 (Handwritten); Interviews with Edna Lewis. Occasional mention of the social activities, election of officers, and programs of the Homemakers, Ladies Aid Society, and Society of Christian Service are in the Kempton columns of the *Oakland* (Maryland) *Republican* during the 1930s and 1940s.

12. Interview with Ethel Fox (widow of Kempton miner), Kempton, Maryland, 2 July 1978.

13. Minutes of Homemakers Club; Interview with Ethel Fox.

14. Interviews with Stanley Turek.

15. Interviews with Edna and Asa Lewis; Interview with Ida Geroski; Interview with Anne Povish Schoen; Interviews with Stanley Turek.

16. Lewis, "Asa Lewis," p. 62; Interviews with Edna and Asa Lewis.

8. Wartime and Winding Down

1. John T. Ward, "Plight of 4 Garrett Towns Illustrates What Happens as Lone Industry Fails," *Baltimore Evening Sun*, 12 May 1950.

2. "Kempton," *Oakland* (Maryland) *Republican*, 2 March 1944; Minutes of Homemakers, Women's Society and Ladies Aid Society.

3. *Oakland* (Maryland) *Republican*, 19 February, 2 July, 16 July, 1 October, 12 November 1942; "Kempton," *Oakland* (Maryland) *Republican*, 15 October 1942.

4. "Kempton," *Oakland* (Maryland) *Republican*, 24 September 1942; "Kempton High Students to Attend Thomas High," *Oakland* (Maryland) *Republican*, 2 July 1942; Interviews with Wanda Corbin (daughter of Gladys Corbin), Kempton, Maryland, 21 October 1976, 3 November 1976, 7 March 1980.

5. Interviews with Martha and Elmer Clark.
6. Interviews with Stanley Turek.
7. Maryland, *Geological Survey, vol. II,* pp. 251-252.
8. Interviews with Harry Buckley (former mine worker and resident of Kempton; former safety engineer, Davis Coal and Coke Company; director, Maryland Bureau of Mines), Kempton, Maryland, 21 November 1977, 9 April 1980, 22 May 1984; Interviews with Elmer Clark.
9. Interview with Mrs. John Cramer (wife of Kempton miner), Bayard, West Virginia, 25 July 1978; Interviews with Mr. and Mrs. Edward E. Sollars; Interviews with Maxine Repetsky.
10. *Oakland* (Maryland) *Republican,* 6 January 1944.
11. *Oakland* (Maryland) Republican, 28 May 1930; *Cumberland Times,* 20 June 1944.
12. Interviews with Maxine Repetsky; *Oakland* (Maryland) *Republican,* 6 November 1944.
13. Interviews with Mrs. Bernard Broll and Richard Broll (miner's widow and son), Kempton, Maryland, 21 October 1976, 11 November 1976; Interviews with Maxine Repetsky.
14. Interviews with Maxine Repetsky.
15. George Kennedy, "Maryland Coal Town Faces Economic Death as Mine—Its Only Industry—Closes," *Washington Evening Star,* 11 May 1950, sec. B; *Oakland* (Maryland) *Republican,* 16 March, 20 April 1950; John T. Ward, five daily articles on unemployment conditions in Allegany and Garrett counties, *Baltimore Evening Sun,* 8-12 May 1950; Interviews with Gladys and Wanda Corbin; Maryland, Bureau of Mines, *Twenty-third Annual Report,* Calendar Year 1945, p. 27; Idem, *Twenty-fourth Annual Report,* Calendar Year 1946, p. 35.
16. Kennedy, "Coal Town."
17. Interviews with Maxine Repetsky.

9. Indian Summer

1. "Steady Private Pay Rolls Sought to Cure Western Maryland Ills." *Baltimore Evening Sun,* 8 May 1950; Kempton School to Garrett County School Superintendent Hardesty, 3 April 1951; Garrett County School Superintendent Hardesty to Patrons, Kempton School, 26 May 1951 (Typewritten).
2. Interviews with Gladys Corbin; Interviews with Maxine Repetsky.
3. Interviews with Richard Broll.
4. Interview with Walter Turek (miner and Kempton landowner), Kempton, Maryland, 27 April 1977.
5. Raymond W. Hicks to Gilbert Gude, 30 November 1976.
6. Interviews with Martha and Elmer Clark.

10. Big Vein Coal Town

1. Hamill T. Kenny, *West Virginia Place Names* (Piedmont, W. Va.: The Place Name Press, 1945), p. 225; Felix G. Robinson, "Coal and Lumber Towns on the Potomac," *Tableland Trails* 2 (Summer 1963):169; Nethken Hill United Methodist Church, *Centennial History, 1875-1975* (Nethken Hill, W. Va.: n.p., 1975), pp. 2, 50-52; Mona Ridder, "Our Mountain Heritage," *News Tribune Mountain Echo— Keyser* (West Virginia), 26 August 1978.

2. Williams, "Davis and Elkins," pp. 58-60.

3. Ridder, "Our Mountain Heritage," 7 October 1978.

4. Pepper, *Life of Davis*, pp. 103-104; Raymond W. Hicks, "The West Virginia Central and Pittsburgh Railway," *The Railway and Locomotive Historical Society* 113 (October 1965):14-15; "The State of Maryland," *Baltimore Sun,* supplement editions, 29-31 March, 11, 29 April 1887; *Cumberland Times*, 26 April, 29 June, 13, 19 July 1887; Callahan, *History of West Virginia*, pp. 474-475.

5. Williams, "Davis and Elkins," pp. 58-60; West Virginia, Board of World's Fair Managers of West Virginia, *Report of the Board of World's Fair Managers of West Virginia, to Gov. William A. MacCorble* (Charleston, W. Va.: Moses W. Donnelly, Public Printer, 1896), p. 47; West Virginia Central, *Seventh Report*, p. 11; Maryland Bureau of Mines, *Tenth Annual Report*, p. 69; "Latest News," *Elk Garden* (West Virginia) *News*, 15 November 1889; West Virginia, Geological Survey, *West Virginia Geological Survey: Mineral and Grant Counties*, by David B. Reger (1924), pp. 15, 19.

6. Williams, "Davis and Elkins," p. 186; Senate Committee on Finance, "Petition Protesting Against a Reduction on the Tariff on Coal," 12 February 1894 (Typewritten); West Virginia, *Mineral and Grant Counties*, pp. 15, 19; Maryland Bureau of Mines, *Tenth Report*, p. 69.

7. Williams, "Davis and Elkins," pp. 58-60.

8. Ridder, "Mountain Heritage," 7 October 1978; Interviews with Roy Wiseman, Elk Garden, West Virginia, 10 May 1976, 10 November 1976, 11 March 1984.

9. "Latest News," *Elk Garden* (West Virginia) *News*, 12 September 1890.

10. Ibid., 3 April 1891.

11. Interviews with Roy Wiseman; Ridder, "Mountain Heritage," 7 October 1978; "Latest News," *Elk Garden* (West Virginia) *News*, 20 June 1890.

12. "Latest News," *Elk Garden* (West Virginia) *News*, 24 April 1891.

13. Kay Denver, *Patent Medicine Picture* (Tombstone, Ariz.: The Tombstone Epitaph, 1968), p. 58; Interviews with Roy Wiseman.

14. Nethken Church, p. 52; Interviews with Roy Wiseman.

15. Interviews with Roy Wiseman.

16. Nethken Church, p. 2; Ridder, "Mountain Heritage," 14 October 1978.

11. An Awful Mine Horror

1. "An Awful Mine Horror," *Oakland* (Maryland) *Republican*, 27 April 1911.

2. West Virginia, Department of Mines, *Annual Report for the Year ending June 30th, 1911*, p. 21.

3. West Virginia, Department of Mines, *Coal Mines in the State of West Virginia*, Twenty-Fourth Annual Report for the year ending June 30, 1906, p. 299.

4. West Virginia, Department of Mines, *Annual Report for the Year ending June 30th, 1910*, p. 105.

5. Department of Mines, *Report for 1911*, p. 87. Interview with William Arnold (former miner in Ott No. 20), Elk Garden, West Virginia, 11 November 1976.

6. "An Awful Mine Horror"; Department of Mines, *Report for 1911*, p. 87; *Piedmont Independent*, 28 April 1911; Interview with George Burdock (former miner and union organizer), Elk Garden, West Virginia, 21 May 1980; "23 Men Entombed," *Baltimore Sun*, 25 April 1911.

7. Interviews with Roy Wiseman; "23 Men Entombed."

8. "20 Bodies Recovered," *Baltimore Sun*, 26 April 1911; "An Awful Mine Horror."

9. "23 Men Entombed."

10. "20 Bodies Recovered."

11. "An Awful Mine Horror"; Department of Mines, *Report for 1911*, p. 288.

12. Ibid.; Interview with William Arnold.

13. "Mine Victims Total 23," *Baltimore Sun*, 27 April 1911; *Charleston (West Virginia) Mail*, 26 April 1911.

14. "Another Tragedy that should not have Occurred," Editorial, *Baltimore Sun*, 26 April 1911.

15. "Was Accident, Says Jury," *Baltimore Sun*, 29 April 1911.

16. Department of Mines, *Report for 1911*, p. 87.

17. Ibid., pp. 21-23.

18. U.S. Department of Interior, Bureau of Mines, "Historical Summary of Coal Mine Explosions in the United States," by Hiram Brown Humphrey, circular 7900 (Washington: Government Printing Office, 1938), p. 49.

19. Matilda Bennear, "Adrift in America," *Employees' Magazine*, July-August 1917.

12. Anxious Change

1. West Virginia University, West Virginia Agricultural Experiment Station, Department of Agricultural Economics and Rural Sociology, *Elk Garden, West Virginia: A Reconnaissance Survey of a Problem Town*, by Ward F. Porter, Jr., Bulletin 355T (June 1952), p. 51.

2. Ibid., p. 45, Table 1.

3. "Breezes from Elk Garden," *Piedmont* (W. Va.) *Herald*, 23 March 1923; reprint Historical Days Edition, 21 June 1973, p. 4.

4. Conley, pp. 190-191.

5. Ridder, "Mountain Heritage," 14 October 1978.

6. West Virginia University, *Elk Garden*, pp. 1-52.

7. Ibid., p. 52.

8. Ibid.

9. Interviews with Jessie Reel (former mayor), Elk Garden, West Virginia, 6 March 1976, 21 October 1976.

10. Interviews with Patricia Droppleman (former mayor), Elk Garden, West Virginia, 21 October 1976, 8 March 1980, 13 August 1980, 11 March 1984.

11. Interview with Clyde Burdock (builder and former teacher), Elk Garden, West Virginia, 21 May 1980; Interviews with Patricia Droppleman; Interviews with Jessie Reel; West Virginia University, *Elk Garden*, p. 43.

13: The Second Passage

1. Michael Shultz, "Mine Drainage Makes Potomac Suffer Greatly," *Baltimore Evening Sun*, 9 August 1977, sec. B.

2. Interview with Blucher Allison (chief engineer, Metikki mine), July 1983.

3. Leo Marx, *The Machine in the Garden: Technology and the Pastoral Ideal in America* (New York: Oxford University Press, 1964).

4. Kennedy, *Blackwater Chronicle*, p. 213.

5. Whitman, "Passage to India," p. 5.

6. Maryland, *An Archeological Study*, p. 1; Interview with Robert D. Wall (archeologist), Maryland Geological Survey, Division of Archeology, Geological Survey Team, 20 May 1983.

7. Interviews with Donna Ware (historian), Maryland Historical Trust, Coal Region Historic Sites Survey, 6 January 1983, 20 May 1983, 13 March 1984.

8. Maryland Department of Natural Resources and the Nature Conservancy, *Executive Summary: The Maryland Natural Heritage Program* (Annapolis: The Maryland Natural Heritage Program, November 1982); Nature Conservancy, Maryland Chapter, "Maryland Natural Areas Campaign: a proposal from the Nature Conservancy," 1982-1985 Priority Natural Area Projects, Bethesda, Md., n.d. (Mimeographed); Interview with Steve Hamblin (director, Maryland Nature Conservancy), Bethesda, Maryland, 15 June 1983.

9. Michael K. Burns, "Peat Firm acquires Bog State wanted Preserved," *Baltimore Sun*, 21 May 1983, sec. C.

10. Maryland Department of Natural Resources, *Maryland Heritage Program*; Nature Conservancy, "Natural Areas Campaign"; Interview with Steve Hamblin.

11. "Conservation Conflict," Editorial, *Oakland* (Maryland) *Republican*, 18 May 1983; "Misleading Information," *Cumberland Evening Times*, Letters to the Editor, 18 May 1983.

12. Burns, "Peat Firm."

13. Interviews with Anthony Abar (director), Maryland Bureau of Mines, 25 February 1983, 1 July 1983, 23 November 1983; U.S. Department of Defense, Army Corps of Engineers, Baltimore District, "North Branch Potomac River Basin Mine Drainage Study," Phase I, Task 3 Report Data Analysis and Definition of Base Conditions (13 September 1976), pp. 247-253.

14. Shultz, "Mine Drainage"; West Virginia, Department of Natural Resources, Division of Water, "North Branch Potomac River Acid Mine Drainage Update," by Monty Edwards (Report to a meeting of the Interstate Commission on the Potomac River Basin, Rockville, Md., 9 December 1982), U.S. Army Corp of Engineers, "North Branch Study."

15. West Virginia, Department of Natural Resources, "North Branch Update"; West Virginia, Department of Natural Resources, Division of Wildlife Resources, "Water Quality of Stony River and North Branch of Potomac River, Grant County," Interoffice Memorandum from Gerald E. Lewis and Virgil Ray to Eli McCoy, 8 November 1982 (Typewritten); Interviews with Russ Newman (superintendent), Army Corp of Engineers, Bloomington Dam and Lake, 23 March 1983, 12 July 1983.

16. Interviews with Anthony Abar.

17. Interviews with Russ Newman; U.S. Department of Defense, Army Corps of Engineers, Baltimore District, "Bloomington Lake," Design Memorandum No. 18, Environmental Analysis, April 1972, p. 38; Mitre Corporation, "An Assessment of the Impact of Improved Water Quality in the North Branch Potomac River Basin," by B. Baratz, R. Cardenas, J. Golden, and L. Thomas (McLean, Va.: Mitre Corporation, May 1974), pp. x-xi.

18. House Committee on Rivers and Harbors, *Potomac River and Tributaries including Occoquan Creek,* 73rd Cong., 1st sess., 1934, H. Doc. 101.

19. Interviews with Russ Newman.

20. Interview with Henry Stetina (general counsel), Interstate Commission on the Potomac River Basin, 22 May 1984.

21. Mitre, "Assessment of Improved Water Quality," p. 4-1.

22. Interview with Blucher Allison.

14. Beyond the Valley

1. U.S. Executive Office of the President, Council on Environmental Quality, Department of State, *Global 2000 Report to the President,* vol. 1 (1980), p. 1.

2. Herman Kahn and Mitchell G. Ford, "Don't Expect Doomsday," *New York Times,* 3 October 1980, sec. A.

3. U.S. Executive Office of the President, Council on Environmental Quality, Department of State, *Global Future: Time to Act* (January 1981), p. xlvi; Anne LaBastille, "Acid Rain: How Great a Menace?" *National Geographic* 160 (November 1981):676.

4. "Acid Rain: The View From Across the Border," *Outdoor America,* September-October 1982, pp. 16-18; Armin Rosenkranz, "The European Conference on Acid Rain," *Environmental Policy and Law* 7 (1981):158-160; LaBastille, 652-681; Larry B. Parker and Robert E. Trumbule, "Mitigating Acid Rain: The Costs for a 10 Million Ton Reduction in SO_2 Emissions," *Materials and Society* 6 (1982): 345-356; Lois R. Ember, "Acid Rain Implicated in Forest Dieback," *Chemical and Engineering News,* 22 November 1982, pp. 25-26; Bette Hileman, "Acid Precipitation," *Environmental Science and Technology* 15 (October 1981): 1119-1124; Russ Hoyle, "Acid Rain: The Silent Plague," *Time,* 8 November 1982, pp. 98-104; Hubert W. Vogelmann, "Catastrophe on Camels Hump," *Natural History* 91 (November 1982): 8-14.

5. Hoyle, p. 104.

6. LaBastille, pp. 662-676; Hoyle, pp. 101-102.

7. Rosenkranz, p. 160.

8. LaBastille, p. 672; See also Vogelmann and Ember.

9. U.S. Executive Office of the President, Council on Environmental Quality, *Global Energy Futures and the Carbon Dioxide Problem* (January 1981); Roger Revelle, "Carbon Dioxide and World Climate," *Scientific American* 247 (August 1982):35-43; House Committee on Science and Technology, *Carbon Dioxide and Climate: The Greenhouse Effect: Hearing before the Subcommittee on Natural Resources, Agriculture Research and Environment and the Subcommittee on Investigations and Oversight* [No. 45], 97th Cong., 1st sess., 31 July 1981.

10. House Committee on Science and Technology, *Carbon Dioxide and Climate: The Greenhouse Effect: Hearing before the Subcommittee on Natural Resources, Agriculture Research and Environment and the Subcommittee on Investigations and Oversight* [No. 115], 97th Cong., 2nd sess., 25 March 1982, pp. 10-11.

11. Sylvan H. Wittwer, "Foreword," in *Carbon Dioxide: Friend or Foe?* by Sherwood B. Idso (Tempe, Ariz.: IBR Press, 1982), pp. vii-ix; House Committee, *Greenhouse Effect*, 25 March 1982, p. 92; CEQ, *Global Energy and Carbon Dioxide*, pp. 60-61, 63.

12. Revelle, p. 38; CEQ, *Global Energy and Carbon Dioxide*, p. 56; Tom Horton, "Deluge Ahead: EPA Study Warns of Rising Sea," *Baltimore Sun*, 1 May 1983, sec. A; Tom Horton, "Projected Risks for Ocean City Range from Greater Erosion to Catastrophe," *Baltimore Sun*, 1 May 1983, sec. A.

13. Revelle, p. 40; CEQ, *Global Energy and Carbon Dioxide*, p. 56.

14. Wittwer, "Foreword"; Revelle.

15. F.K. Hare, "The Buildup of CO_2," review of *Carbon Dioxide Review* (1982), ed. William C. Clark, *Science,* 21 January 1983, p. 283.

16. Wil Lepkowski, "Ideological Debate rages over Global 2000 Report," *Chemical and Engineering News,* 13 June 1983, p. 20.

17. Eugene F. Mallove, "Our Universe, Created from Nothing," *Washington Post,* 3 June 1984, sec B.

18. Hulbert, *Washington and the West*, pp. 194-195.

A Special Note About John Vachon, pp. 79-94.

John Vachon was 25 years old when he visited Kempton and it would be another two years before he was to be made a full-fledged member of the Farm Security photo team. Just out of college and in desperate need of a job, he had gone to work in 1936 in the historical section of FSA's information department as an assistant messenger. The job title was a misnomer. Roy Stryker, the unit's catalytic director, kept him busy mostly copying captions on the backs of 8" × 10" photographs and stamping them with the names of the photographers. (In time he became responsible for organizing and classifying the entire FSA collection, which eventually included about 270,000 negatives.) It was during this period that he came not only to recognize the distinctive qualities in the work of each photographer but to appreciate the common values that ran through the entire FSA project. In college, Vachon had majored in English literature. He understood the importance of theme. Long before he himself pressed a shutter he knew better than most exactly what it was that would produce in the FSA collection such an extraordinarily coherent statement about America in the Great Depression.

One day Vachon told Stryker that he thought there were a lot of scenes in Washington that should be photographed for the files. Stryker responded by suggesting that he borrow a camera and give it a try. He did. No less an artist than Ben Shahn told Vachon how to focus the Leica and which button to push. Shortly thereafter Walker Evans persuaded him to exchange the Leica for an 8″ × 10″ view camera, and for the first several years he was, as he said later, "sedulously aping the masters." But in 1939, when the pictures of Kempton were taken, John Vachon was emerging with a style all his own, photographing "only what pleased or astonished my eye, and only in the way I saw it." In their compassion and simplicity, his photographs still showed the influence of Dorothea Lange, and in the purity of their composition that of Walker Evans, but what was beginning to come through more strongly was a unique sensitivity, a quality that viewers recognized as both personal and universal. In Kempton, Vachon was learning to use the camera unobtrusively and shaping his conviction that photography was best as an interpretive medium when it remained a medium of straight reporting. It was a philosophy that clearly invested all his work after World War II, most of which was done as a staff photographer for LOOK magazine.

Vachon died of cancer in 1975, a month shy of his sixty-first birthday. The pictures on pages 79–94 are from the FSA collection at the Library of Congress.

— *Calvin Kytle*

Sources

"Tribute to a Man, an Era, an Art." Commentary by John Vachon in *Harpers*, September 1973, pp. 96-99.

Kernan, Sean. "John Vachon — Profile of a Magazine Photographer." *Camera 35*, December 1971, pp. 31 + .

Vachon, Brian. "John Vachon: A Remembrance." *American Photographer*, October 1979, pp. 34 + .

Bibliography

Abar, Anthony (director). Maryland Bureau of Mines. Interviews, 25 February 1983, 1 July 1983, 23 November 1983.

"Acid Rain: The View From Across the Border." *Outdoor America*, September-October 1982, pp. 16-18.

Allison, Blucher (chief engineer, Metikk mine). Interview, July 1983.

Ambler, Charles H. *A History of Education in West Virginia: From Early Colonial Times to 1949.* Huntington, W.Va.: Standard Printing and Publishing Co., 1951.

Ambler, Charles H. *West Virginia—The Mountain State.* New York: Prentice-Hall Inc., 1940.

Andrews, Henry N., Jr. *Ancient Plants and the World They Lived In.* Ithaca, N.Y.: Comstock Publishing Co., 1947.

Andrews, Henry N., Jr. *Studies in Paleobotany.* New York: John Wiley and Sons, Inc., 1961.

Arnold, William (former miner in Ott No. 20). Elk Garden, West Virginia. Interview, 11 November 1976.

Baltimore American. *A History of the City of Baltimore.* Baltimore: Press of Williams and Wilkins Co., 1902.

Baltimore Evening Sun, 8-12 May, 1950; 9 August 1977.

Baltimore Sun, 29-31 March, 11, 29 April 1887; 25-27, 29 April 1911; 1 March 1916; 1, 21 May 1983; 15 November 1983.

Baltimore Sunday Sun, 2 October 1977.

Bennett, Kyle (son of former Kempton miner). Kempton, Maryland. Interview, 7 March 1980.

"Bloomington at the Mouth of Savage." *Glades Star* 1 (30 September 1949):361-363, 365.

"Breezes from Elk Garden." *Piedmont* (W. Va.) *Herald*, 23 March 1923; reprint Historical Days Edition, 21 June 1973.

Broll, Mrs. Bernard and Richard (miner's widow and son). Kempton, Maryland. Interviews, 21 October 1976, 11 November 1976.

Brooks, W.E. *The Northwest Turnpike and West Virginia.* A Newcomen Address published under the auspices of the American Branch of the Newcomen Society. Princeton, N.J.: Princeton University Press, 1943.

Buckley, Harry (former mine worker and resident of Kempton; former safety engineer, Davis Coal and Coke Company; director, Maryland Bureau of Mines). Kempton, Maryland. Interviews, 21 November 1977, 9 April 1980, 22 May 1984.

Burdock, Clyde (builder and former teacher). Elk Garden, West Virginia. Interview, 21 May 1980.

Burdock, Mr. and Mrs. George (former miner and union organizer, and his wife, a former teacher). Elk Garden, West Virginia. Interview, 21 May 1980.

Calandralla, Ralph (physician). Kitzmiller, Maryland. Interview, 12 November 1976.

Calderwood, Paul T. "Community Schools of Garrett County." *Glades Star* 4 (March 1977):744-747.

Caldwell, Walter. *Coal Company Scrip*. Montgomery, W. Va.: Ware Printing Company, 1969.

Callahan, James Morton. *History of West Virginia*. Chicago and New York: American Historical Society, Inc., 1923.

Callahan, James Morton. *Semi-Centennial History of West Virginia*. Morgantown, W. Va.: Semi-Centennial Commission of West Virginia, 1913.

Carbone, Frank Anthony (Tony) (former miner). Kempton, Maryland. Interview, 3 July 1977.

Carpenter, Charles. "West Virginia Buffalo Trails." *The West Virginia Review* 8 (July 1931):323-333, 348.

Charleston (West Virginia) *Mail*. 26 April 1911.

Ciellers, Ernest (former Kempton miner) to his niece, n.d.

Clark, Elmer (retired miner). Kempton, Maryland. Interviews, 11 June 1977, 27 August 1977, 15 October 1977, 21 October 1977, 25 July 1978.

Clark, Martha ("Twila") (miner's widow). Kempton, Maryland. Interviews, 7 March 1980, 5 March 1984, 10 March 1984.

Clark, Vera (former resident). Elk Garden, West Virginia. Interview, n.d.

Clarkson, Roy B. *Tumult on the Mountains: Lumbering in West Virginia— 1770-1920*. Parsons, W. Va.: McClain Printing Company, 1964.

Comp, Frances. "Doctors of Deer Park." *Glades Star* 2 (30 September 1951): 109-110.

Conley, Phil. *History of the West Virginia Coal Industry*. Charleston, W. Va.: Education Foundation, Inc., 1960.

Corbin, Gladys (miner's widow). Kempton, Maryland. Interviews, 21 October 1976, 3 November 1976, 7 March 1980.

Corbin, Wanda (daughter of Gladys Corbin). Kempton, Maryland. Interviews, 21 October 1976, 3 November 1976, 7 March 1980.

Corliss, Frank R., Jr. "Folly Run Cairn No. 1, 18-Ga-54." *The West Virginia Archeologist* 16 (December 1963):1-4.

Corliss, Frank R., Jr., and Henry T. Wright III. "A Preliminary Analysis of Recent Excavations in the Upper Potomac Valley." *The Journal of the Archaeological Society of Maryland, Inc.* 3 (September 1967): 145-152.

Cowling, Ellis (director). U.S. Department of Agriculture. National Atmospheric Deposition Program. Interview, 22 April 1983.

Cramer, Mrs. John (wife of Kempton miner). Bayard, West Virginia. Interview, 25 July 1978.

Crowley, J.E. *This Sheba, Self: The Conceptualization of Economic Life in Eighteenth-Century America*. Baltimore and London: The Johns Hopkins University Press, 1974.

Cumberland Evening Times. Letters to the Editor, 18 May 1983.

Cumberland Times, 27 October 1884; 26 April, 29 June, 13, 19 July 1887; 20 June 1944.

Davidson, Marshall B., ed. *Notable American Houses*. New York: American Heritage Publishing Co., Inc. 1971.

Davis Coal and Coke Company. *Davis Coal News*. Baltimore, Md. January 1933-December 1935.

Davis Coal and Coke Company. *Employees' Magazine*. Cumberland, Md. 2 July 1917; 2 November 1917.

Davis Coal and Coke Company. *Our Own People: The Monthly Magazine of the Davis Coal and Coke Company*. Cumberland, Md. January 1918-December 1919.

Davis, Henry G. "National and State Politics." Speech delivered at Mineral County Convention, Mineral County, W.Va., 15 August 1874.

"Davis Journal." *Glades Star* 2 (31 December 1951):125.

"Deer Park Hotel." *Glades Star* 2 (31 December 1951): 122-125.

Dempsey, Harvey (miner). Elk Garden, West Virginia. Interview, 21 May 1980.

Denver, Kay. *Patent Medicine Picture*. Tombstone, Ariz.: The Tombstone Epitaph, 1968.

Detzer, Dorothy. *Appointment on the Hill*. New York: Henry Holt and Co., 1948.

Dodge, J.R. *West Virginia: Its Farms and Forests, Mines and Oil-Wells*. Philadelphia: J.B. Lippincott & Co., 1865.

"Domestic Art Items and Gossip." *Cosmopolitan Art Journal* 1 (September 1858): 207.

Droppleman, Patricia (former mayor). Elk Garden, West Virginia. Interviews, 21 October 1976, 8 March 1980, 13 August 1980, 11 March 1984.

Elk Garden (West Virginia) *News*, 15 November 1889; 20 June, 12 September 1890; 3, 24 April 1891.

Ember, Lois R. "Acid Rain Implicated in Forest Dieback." *Chemical and Engineering News*, 22 November 1982, pp. 25-26.

Encyclopaedia Britannica, 15th ed. S.v. "Southwest American Indians." By Laura Thompson.

"Extinct Animals of Garrett County." *Glades Star* 2 (31 March 1952):139-142.

Fairbanks, W.L. and W.S. Hamill. *The Coal Mining Industry of Maryland*. Baltimore: Maryland Development Bureau of the Baltimore Association of Commerce, 1932.

"The Fairfax Stone." *Glades Star* 2 (March 1958):435-439.

"Fifth Annual Tour of the Garrett County Historical Society." *Glades Star* 2 (December 1959):545-548.

"First Settlers of the Glades Country." *Glades Star* 1 (2 July 1941):9, 11–13.

Fox, Ethel (widow of Kempton miner). Kempton, Maryland. Interview, 2 July 1978.

Garrett County (Maryland) Board of School Commissioners. Minutes of Meetings, 1873-1916. (Handwritten)

Geroski, Francis (son of Ida Geroski). Kempton, Maryland. Interview, 20 November 1977.

Geroski, Ida (miner's widow). Kempton, Maryland. Interview, 20 November 1977.

Geroski, John (son of Ida Geroski). Kempton, Maryland. Interview, 20 November 1977.

Gibbs, Roy (retired mine employee). Kempton, Maryland. Interview, 21 October 1976.

"Gorman—1928." *Glades Star* 2 (30 June 1953):193-196.

Graham, Frank, Jr. *Potomac: The Nation's River*. Philadelphia and New York: J.B. Lippincott Co., 1976.

Gutheim, Frederick. *The Potomac*. New York: Holt, Rinehart and Winston, 1974.

Hamblin, Steve (director, Maryland Nature Conservancy). Bethesda, Maryland. Interview, 15 June 1983.

Hardesty, Garrett County School Superintendent, to Patrons, Kempton School, 26 May 1951. (Typewritten.)

Hare, F. K. "The Buildup of CO_2." Review of *Carbon Dioxide Review*, 1982. Ed. William C. Clark. *Science*, 21 January 1983, p. 283.

Harvey, Katherine A. *The Best Dressed Miners: Life and Labor in the Maryland Coal Region, 1835-1910*. Ithaca: Cornell University Press, 1969.

Helvey, David (project leader). U.S. Department of Agriculture. National Atmospheric Deposition Program. Interview, 22 April 1983.

Herbstritt, James T. "Bonnie Brook: A Multicomponent Aboriginal Locus in West-Central Pennsylvania." *Pennsylvania Archaeologist* 51 (September 1981): 1-59.

Hicks, Raymond W. to Gilbert Gude, 30 November 1976.

Hicks, Raymond W. "The West Virginia Central and Pittsburgh Railway." *The Railway and Locomotive Historical Society* 113 (October 1965):6-31.

"High Speed Shaft Hoist Increases Output". *The Coal Industry* 1 (February 1918): 48-51.

Hileman, Bette. "Acid Precipitation." *Environmental Science and Technology* 15 (October 1981):1119-1124.

Hilton, William, Jr. and Katie (former miner and his wife). Kempton, Maryland. Interviews, 27 August 1977, 15 October 1977.

Hobbs, Horace P., Jr. *Pioneers of the Potowmack*. Ann Arbor, Mich.: University Microfilms, Inc., 1964.

Hollander, Ellie. "DOE Takes the Lead in CO_2 Research." *Electric Power Research Institute Journal* 7 (June 1982):34-36.

Hoye, Charles E. "Garrett County History of Pioneer Families: CVI. The Bruce Family." *Oakland* (Maryland) *Mountain Democrat*, n.d.

Hoyle, Russ. "Acid Rain: The Silent Plague." *Time*, 8 November 1982, pp. 98-104.

Hulbert, Archer Butler. *Historic Highways of America*. Vol. 1, *Paths of the Mound-Building Indians and Great Game Animals*. New York: AMS Press, 1971.

Hulbert, Archer Butler. *Historic Highways of America*. Vol. 12, *Pioneer Roads and Experiences of Travelers* (II). New York: AMS Press, 1971.

Hulbert, Archer Butler. *Washington and the West: Being George Washington's Diary of September, 1784. Kept during his journey into the Ohio Basin in* the interest of a commercial union between the Great Lakes and the Potomac River—And a commentary upon the same by Archer Butler Hulbert. New York: The Century Co., 1905.

Idleman, D.W. "Gormania." Glades Star 2 (30 June 1953):197-198.

Idleman, D.W. "The Schaeffers." Glades Star 2 (30 June 1953):201-203.

Idso, Sherwood B. Carbon Dioxide: Friend or Foe? Tempe, Ariz.: IBR Press, 1982.

Illinois. Department of Registration and Education. Division of the Illinois State Museum. Leaves and Stems from Fossil Forests: A Handbook of the Paleobotanical Collections in the Illinois State Museum. By Raymond E. Janssen. Popular Science Series No. 1. Springfield, Ill., 1957.

The Johns Hopkins University. The Isaiah Bowman Department of Geography. "Salvage Archeology of the Bloomington Project North Branch of the Potomac River: Maryland and West Virginia." Baltimore: December 1967. (Mimeographed.)

Kempton (Maryland) Homemakers Club. Minutes of Monthly Meetings, 1938-1943. (Handwritten.)

Kempton (Maryland) Ladies Aid Society. Minutes of Monthly Meetings, 1933. (Handwritten.)

Kempton (Maryland) Women's Society of Christian Service in the Local Church. Minutes of Monthly Meetings, 1943-1944 (Handwritten.)

Kempton School to Garrett County School Superintendent Hardesty, 3 April 1951.

Kennedy, Philip Pendleton [The Clerke of Oxenforde]. The Blackwater Chronicle. New York: Redfield, 1853.

Kenny, Hamill T. West Virginia Place Names. Piedmont, W. Va.: The Place Name Press, 1945.

Kimball, Fiske. Domestic Architecture of the American Colonies and of the Early Republic. New York: Dover Publications, Inc., 1950.

Koch, Michael. The Shay Locomotive. Denver: World Press, Inc., 1971.

Korling, Torkel. Wild Plants in Flower II: The Boreal Forests and Borders. Dundee, Ill.: The Lakeside Press, 1973.

Kouwenhoven, John A. Made in America. Garden City, N. Y.: Doubleday and Company, Inc., 1948.

Kurth, Mrs. James A. (Wanda) (former resident). Elk Garden, West Virginia. Interview, 13 December 1976.

LaBastille, Anne. "Acid Rain: How Great a Menace?" National Geographic 160 (November 1981):652-681.

Lepkowski, Wil. "Ideological Debate rages over Global 2000 Report." Chemical and Engineering News, 13 June 1983, p. 20.

Lewis, Asa. "Asa Lewis, 1887-1977." Glades Star 5 (March 1978):58-63.

Lewis, Asa (former principal of Kempton School). Kempton, Maryland. Interview, 11 November 1976.

Lewis, Edna (widow of former principal, Kempton School). Kempton, Maryland. Interviews, 11 November 1976, 21 November 1977, 8 March 1980.

"Loose Change." Regardie's, November-December 1981, p. 13.

"McCullough's Pack Horse Path." Glades Star 1 (30 September 1948): 297-299.

McHarg, Ian. *Design with Nature*. Garden City, N.Y.: Natural History Press, 1969.

Mallott, Floyd E. *Studies in Brethren History*. Elgin, Ill.: Brethren Publishing House, 1954.

Marx, Leo. *The Machine in the Garden: Technology and the Pastoral Ideal in America*. New York: Oxford University Press, 1964.

Maryland. *Annual Report of the Mine Inspector for Allegany and Garrett Counties, Maryland.* 1 May 1914 to 1 May 1915.

Maryland. *Annual Report of the Mining Inspector*. From 1 May 1915 to 1 May 1917.

Maryland. Bureau of Mines. *Tenth Annual Report*. Calendar Year 1932.

Maryland. Bureau of Mines. *Twenty-third Annual Report*. Calendar Year 1945.

Maryland. Bureau of Mines. *Twenty-fourth Annual Report*. Calendar Year 1946.

Maryland. Department of Economic and Community Development. *Maryland Historical Atlas*. Washington: Raymond, Parish, Pine and Plavnick, 1973.

Maryland. Department of Geology Mines and Water Resources. *Refractory Clays of the Maryland Coal Measures*. Baltimore: Waverly Press, 1950.

Maryland. Department of Natural Resources. Maryland Geological Survey. Division of Archeology. *An Archeological Study of the Western Maryland Coal Region: The Prehistoric Resources*. By Robert D. Wall. Frostburg, Md.: Maryland Geological Survey, December 1981.

Maryland. Department of Natural Resources and the Nature Conservancy. *Executive Summary: The Maryland Natural Heritage Program*. Annapolis: The Maryland Natural Heritage Program, November 1982.

Maryland. Maryland Geological Survey. *Caves of Maryland*. By Richard Franz and Dennis Slifer. Educational Series no. 3. 1971.

Maryland. Maryland Geological Survey. *Maryland Geological Survey: Garrett County*. Baltimore: The Johns Hopkins University Press, 1902.

Maryland. Maryland Geological Survey. *Maryland Geological Survey. Vol. II*. Baltimore: The Johns Hopkins University Press, 1922.

Maryland. Maryland Geological Survey. *Report on the Coals of Maryland*. Baltimore: The Johns Hopkins University Press, 1905.

Maryland. *Maryland Manual*, 1919-1920.

Maryland v. West Virginia. 217 U.S. 1-47, 1910.

Mayer-Oakes, William J. *Prehistory of the Upper Ohio Valley; An Introductory Archeological Study*. Anthropological Series no. 2. *Annals of Carnegie Museum* 34 (1955).

Members of The Johns Hopkins University and Others. *Maryland, its Resources, Industries, and Institutions*. Baltimore: The Sun Job Printing Office, 1893.

Miller, Arnold (former miner). Elk Garden, West Virginia. Interview, 11 November 1976.

Mitre Corporation. "An Assessment of the Impact of Improved Water Quality in the North Branch Potomac River Basin." By B. Baratz, R. Cardenas, J. Golden, and L. Thomas. McLean, Va.: Mitre Corporation, May 1974.

Morrison, Charles. *The Fairfax Line*. Parsons, W. Va.: McClain Printing Company, 1970.

Muma, Martin H. "Maryland's Largest Shelter Cave." *Maryland: A Journal of Natural History* 14 (January 1944):62-65.

Nature Conservancy, Maryland Chapter. "Maryland Natural Areas Campaign: a proposal from the Nature Conservancy," 1982-1985 Priority Natural Area Projects. Bethesda, Md., n.d. (Mimeographed.)

Nethken Hill United Methodist Church. *Centennial History, 1875-1975*. Nethken Hill, W. Va.: n.p., 1975.

Newman, Russ (superintendent). Army Corp of Engineers. Bloomington Dam and Lake. Interviews, 23 March 1983, 12 July 1983.

New York Times, 3 October 1980.

Oakland (Maryland) *Republican*, 16 March-6 July 1911; 24 July 1913; 23 July 1914; 2 March 1916; 16 February 1922; 6, 13 March, 3, 10 April, 28 August 1924; 28 May, 13 November, 11 December 1930; 17 November 1932; 12 November 1936; 19 February, 2, 16 July, 24 September, 1, 15 October, 12 November 1942; 6 January, 2 March, 6, 16 November 1944; 16 March, 20 April 1950; 18 May 1983.

Oxford Dictionary of the Christian Church, 2nd ed. S .v. "Tunkers."

Parker, Glen Lawhon. *The Coal Industry*. Washington: American Council on Public Affairs, 1940.

Parker, Larry B. and Robert E. Trumbule. "Mitigating Acid Rain: The Costs for a 10 Million Ton Reduction in SO_2 Emissions." *Materials and Society* 6 (1982):345-356.

Parsons (West Virginia) *Advocate*, 2 March 1916; 27 April 1950.

Pennsylvania. The Pennsylvania Historical and Museum Commission. *Indian Paths of Pennsylvania*. By Paul A.W. Wallace. Harrisburg: The Pennsylvania Historical and Museum Commission, 1965.

Pepper, Charles M. *The Life and Times of Henry Gassaway Davis*. New York: The Century Company, 1920.

Pepper, George H. "Ceremonial Objects and Ornaments from Pueblo Bonito, New Mexico." *American Anthropologist*, n.s., 7 (April-June 1905):183-197.

Piedmont Independent, 28 April 1911.

"Pioneer Path." *Glades Star* 5 (March 1978):68-69.

Possiel, Bill. "Campaign Underway to Abolish Synthetic Fuels Corporation." *Audubon Naturalist News* 9 (March 1983):3.

Ranger, Ralph Daniel. *Pacific Coast Shay: Strong Man of the Woods*. San Marino, Calif.: Golden West Books, 1964.

Reel, Jessie (former mayor). Elk Garden, West Virginia. Interviews, 6 March 1976, 21 October 1976.

Repetsky, Maxine Corbin (miner's widow and lifelong resident of Kempton). Kempton, Maryland. Interviews, 15 October 1977, 7 March 1980, 21 February 1983, 23 March 1983, 8 March 1984.

Revelle, Roger. "Carbon Dioxide and World Climate." *Scientific American* 247 (August 1982):35-43.

Ridder, Mona (columnist). *News Tribune Mountain Echo—Keyser* (West Virginia). Elk Garden, West Virginia, Interview, 12 December 1983, 10 March 1984.

Ridder, Mona. "Our Mountain Heritage." *News Tribune Mountain Echo—Keyser* (West Virginia). Nine weekly articles, 19 August 1978-14 October 1978.

Robinson, Felix G. "City Boy Makes Good in the Country." *Glades Star* 3 (December 1961):129-131, 142-144, 3 (March 1962):146-147, 149-151.

Robinson, Felix G. "Coal and Lumber Towns on the Potomac." *Tableland Trails* 2 (Summer 1963):169.

Robinson, Felix G. "Davis, West Virginia: Village of Undying Hope." *Tableland Trails* 1 (Spring 1953):25-47.

Roe, Frank Gilbert. *The North American Buffalo: A Critical Study of the Species in its Wild State.* 2nd ed. Toronto and Buffalo: University of Toronto Press, 1970.

Roseboom, Eugene H. *A History of Presidential Elections.* London: The Macmillan Company, Collier-Macmillan Ltd., 1970.

Rosenkranz, Armin. "The European Conference on Acid Rain." *Environmental Policy and Law* 7 (1981):158-160.

Ryan, Leslie (miner's wife and clerk in Kempton company store). Kempton, Maryland. Interview, 2 July 1978.

Santmire, H. Paul. *Brother Earth.* New York: Thomas Nelson, Inc., 1970.

Sawyers, Charles (former mine boss with the Davis Coal and Coke Company). Interview, 12 November 1976.

Schaeffer, John Randolph. *From Baltimore to Charleston.* Gormania, W. Va.: n.p., 1906.

Schaeffer, John Randolph. *Over the Alleghenies by the Northwestern Turnpike— Now the Great Scenic Federal Highway.* Gormania, W. Va.: n.p., 1928.

Scharf, J. Thomas. *History of Western Maryland.* 2 vols. Philadelphia: Louis H. Everts, 1882.

Schlossnagle, Stephen and the Garrett County Bicentennial Committee. *Garrett County: A History of Maryland's Tableland.* Parsons, W. Va.: McClain Printing Company, 1978.

Schoen, Anne Povish (attended Kempton Elementary School). Kempton, Maryland. Interview, 13 September 1977.

Selders, Rodney W. "Garrett County Coal Industry." *Glades Star* 2 (31 December 1953):225-235.

Sevareid, Eric. "Up with the Work Ethic." *Think*, July 1976, pp. 22-23.

Seward, A.C. *Plant Life through the Ages: A Geological and Botanical Retrospect.* London: Cambridge University Press, 1931.

Sheer, Daniel P. and Daniel C. Harris. "Acidity Control in the North Branch Potomac." *Journal Water Pollution Control Federation* 54 (November 1982):1441-1446.

Smithsonian Institution. Bureau of American Ethnology. *42d Annual Report of the Bureau of American Ethnology: 1924-1925.* Washington: U.S. Government Printing Office, 1928.

Smithsonian Institution. Bureau of American Ethnology. "Indian Trails of the Southeast." By William E. Myer in *42d Annual Report of the Bureau of American Ethnology.* Washington: U.S. Government Printing Office, 1928.

Smithsonian Institution. Bureau of American Ethnology. "Two Summers' Work in Pueblo Ruins." By Jesse Walter Fewkes in *22d Annual Report of the Bureau of American Ethnology.* Washington: U.S. Government Printing Office, 1904.

Sollars, Mr. and Mrs. Edward E. (former Kempton miner, son of company doctor, and his wife). Kempton, Maryland. Interviews, 5 January 1978, 16 June 1978.

Spitzer, Gallery (former employee). Western Maryland Railroad. Interview, 21 October 1976.

Stetina, Henry (general counsel). Interstate Commission on the Potomac River Basin. Interview, 22 May 1984.

Strothers, David H. [Porte, Crayon]. *Virginia Illustrated*. New York: Harpers and Brothers, 1957.

Thunderbird Research Corporation. "Bloomington Lake Reservoir: A Cultural Resources Reconnaissance." By Kathleen Quinn and William Gardner, June 1979. (Mimeographed.)

"A Traveler over McCullough's Path." *Glades Star* 1 (30 September 1948):299.

Trumbule, Robert E. and Larry B. Parker. "Acid Rain: Clouds Coal–Nuclear Issue." *Energy Management* 9 (March 1983):23-26.

Turek, Stanley (Kempton miner and union president). Kempton, Maryland. Interviews, 2 July 1978, 13 July 1978, 19 March 1979.

Turek, Mr. and Mrs. Walter (miner and Kempton landowner and his wife). Kempton, Maryland. Interview, 27 August 1977.

United Mine Workers of America. Local Union No. 4113. "Treasurer's Cash Book." Kempton, Maryland, 1934-1950.

U.S. Congress. House. Committee on Energy and Commerce. *The Strategic Future: Anticipating Tomorrow's Crises.* 97th Cong., 1st sess., August 1981. Committee Print 97-U.

U.S. Congress. House. Committee on Rivers and Harbors. *Potomac River and Tributaries including Occoquan Creek.* 73rd Cong., 1st sess., 1934. H. Doc. 101.

U.S. Congress. House. Committee on Roads and Canals. *Chesapeake and Ohio Canal.* 19th Cong., 1st sess., 22 May 1826. H. Rept. 228.

U.S. Congress. House. Committee on Science and Technology. *Carbon Dioxide and Climate: The Greenhouse Effect: Hearing before the Subcommittee on Natural Resources, Agriculture Research and Environment and the Subcommittee on Investigations and Oversight* [No. 45], 97th Cong., 1st sess., 31 July 1981.

U.S. Congress. House. Committee on Science and Technology. *Carbon Dioxide and Climate: The Greenhouse Effect: Hearing before the Subcommittee on Natural Resources, Agriculture Research and Environment and the Subcommittee on Investigations and Oversight* [No. 115]. 97th Cong., 2nd sess., 25 March 1982.

U.S. Congress. Library of Congress. Congressional Research Service. Science Policy Research Division. "Carbon Dioxide and Climate." By John R. Justus, November 1982. (Mimeographed.)

U.S. Congress. Library of Congress. Congressional Research Service. Science Policy Research Division. "Tropical Forests: The Deforestation Problem, Atmospheric Carbon Dioxide and Climate." By John R. Justus, 10 July 1980. (Mimeographed.)

U.S. Congress. Senate. *Biographical Directory of the American Congress.* 92nd Cong., 1st sess., 1971. S. Doc. 92-8.

U.S. Congress. Senate. Committee on Finance. "Petition Protesting Against a Reduction on the Tariff on Coal," 12 February 1894. (Typewritten.)

U.S. Department of Agriculture. Farm Security Administration. "Farm Security Collection Negatives." By John A. Vachon. 1357M-1387M; 8970-8999; 60,000-60,009.

U.S. Department of Defense. Army Corp of Engineers. Baltimore District. "Bloomington Lake." Design Memorandum No. 18, Environmental Analysis, April 1972.

U.S. Department of Defense. Army Corps of Engineers. Baltimore District. "North Branch Potomac River Basin Mine Drainage Study." Phase I, Task 3 Report Data Analysis and Definition of Base Conditions, 13 September 1976.

U.S. Department of Interior. Bureau of Mines. "Historical Summary of Coal Mine Explosions in the United States." By Hiram Brown Humphrey. Circular 7900. Washington: Government Printing Office, 1938.

U.S. Department of Interior. Geological Survey. *Upper Paleozoic Floral Zones and Floral Provinces of the United States.* By Charles B. Read and Sergius H. Mamay. Geological Survey Professional Paper 454—K. Washington: U.S. Government Printing Office, 1964.

U.S. Department of Interior. National Park Service. *The National Register of Historic Places—1976.*

U.S. Environmental Protection Agency. Office of Research and Monitoring. "Testing Program for Mining Coal in Oxygen Free Atmosphere," January 1976.

U.S. Executive Office of the President. Council on Environmental Quality. *Global Energy Futures and the Carbon Dioxide Problem.* January 1981.

U.S. Executive Office of the President. Council on Environmental Quality. Department of State. *Global Future: Time to Act.* January 1981.

U.S. Executive Office of the President. Council on Environmental Quality. Department of State. *Global 2000 Report to the President.* Vol. 1. 1980.

Veech, James. *The Monongahela of Old; or, Historical Sketches of South-Western Pennsylvania to the Year 1800.* Pittsburgh: By the Author, 1858-1892.

Vogelmann, Hubert W. "Catastrophe on Camels Hump." *Natural History* 91 (November 1982):8-14.

Walker, J.J. (former superintendent with the Hamil Coal Company). Kitzmiller, Maryland. Interview, 21 October 1976.

Wall, Robert D. "Excavations at the Cresaptown Site in the Upper Potomac Valley." Paper presented at the fall meeting of the Potomac River Basin Consortium, Frostburg, Md., October 1983.

Wall, Robert D. to Gilbert Gude, January 1984.

Wall, Robert D. (archeologist). Maryland Geological Survey. Division of Archeology. Geological Survey Team. Interviews, 20 May 1983, 2 June 1984.

Ward, John T. Five daily articles on unemployment conditions in Allegany and Garrett counties. *Baltimore Evening Sun,* 8-12 May 1950.

Ware, Donna (historian). Maryland Historical Trust. Coal Region Historic Sites Survey. Interviews, 6 January 1983, 20 May 1983; 13 March 1984.

Washington Evening Star, 11 May 1950.

Washington Post, 3 June 1984.

Westminster Dictionary of Church History, 1971 ed. S.v. "Brethren (Dunkers)."

West Virginia. Board of World's Fair Managers of West Virginia. *Report of the Board of World's Fair Managers of West Virginia, to Gov. William A. MacCorble.* Charleston, W. Va.: Moses W. Donnelly, Public Printer, 1896.

West Virginia Central and Pittsburg Railway Company. *First Report, January 1st, 1882*. Washington: R.O. Polkinhorn, Printer, 1882.

West Virginia Central and Pittsburg Railway Company. *Report of the President, October 17, 1882*. Baltimore: n.p., 1882.

West Virginia Central and Pittsburg Railway Company. *Second Annual Report, January 8, 1884*. Baltimore: Wm. J.C. Dulany and Co., 1884.

West Virginia Central and Pittsburg Railway Company. *Third Annual Report, January 27, 1885*. Baltimore: Wm. J.C. Dulany and Co., 1885.

West Virginia Central and Pittsburg Railway Company. *Fourth Annual Report, January 26, 1886*. Baltimore: American Steam Job Press, 1886.

West Virginia Central and Pittsburg Railway Company. *Fifth Annual Report, January 25, 1887*. Baltimore: Wm. J.C. Dulany and Co., 1887.

West Virginia Central and Pittsburg Railway Company. *Sixth Annual Report, January 24, 1888*. Baltimore: Press of Guggenheimer, Weil and Co., 1888.

West Virginia Central and Pittsburg Railway Company. *Seventh Annual Report, January 22, 1889*. Baltimore: Wm. J.C. Dulany and Co., 1889.

West Virginia Central and Pittsburg Railway Company, *Ninth Annual Report, January 27, 1891*. Baltimore: Wm. J.C. Dulany Co., 1891.

West Virginia Central and Pittsburg Railway Company. *Eleventh Annual Report, Six Months ended June 30, 1892*. Cumberland: Press of Frank B. Jenvey, 1892.

West Virginia Central and Pittsburg Railway Company. *Thirteenth Annual Report, Fiscal Year ended June 30, 1894*. Cumberland: Press of Frank B. Jenvey, 1894.

West Virginia Central and Pittsburg Railway Company. *Fourteenth Annual Report, Fiscal Year ended June 30, 1895*. Baltimore: Wm. J.A. Dulany Co., 1895.

West Virginia Central and Pittsburg Railway Company. *Sixteenth Annual Report, Fiscal Year ended June 30, 1897*. Baltimore: Press of the Baltimore American, 1897.

West Virginia Central and Pittsburg Railway Company. *Seventeenth Annual Report, Fiscal Year ended June 30, 1898*. Baltimore: Press of the Baltimore American, 1898.

West Virginia Central and Pittsburg Railway Company. *Eighteenth Annual Report, Fiscal Year ended June 30, 1899*. Baltimore: Wm. J.C. Dulany Co., 1899.

West Virginia Central and Pittsburg Railway Company. *Nineteenth Annual Report, Fiscal Year ended June 30, 1900*. Washington: Gibson Bros., Printers and Bookbinders, 1900.

West Virginia Central and Pittsburg Railway Company. *Twentieth Annual Report, Fiscal Year ended June 30, 1901*. Washington: Gibson Bros., Printers and Bookbinders, 1901.

West Virginia Central and Pittsburgh Railway Company. *West Virginia Central and Pittsburgh Railway*. Cumberland, Md.: The Independent Job Room, 1899.

West Virginia. Department of Mines. *Annual Report for the Year ending June 30th, 1910*.

West Virginia. Department of Mines. *Annual Report for the Year ending June 30th, 1911*.

West Virginia. Department of Mines. *Annual Report for the Year ending June 30th, 1912*.

West Virginia. Department of Mines. *Coal Mines in the State of West Virginia.* Twenty-Fourth Annual Report for the year ending June 30, 1906.

West Virginia. Department of Natural Resources. Division of Water. "North Branch Potomac River Acid Mine Drainage Update." By Monty Edwards. Report to a meeting of the Interstate Commission on the Potomac River Basin, Rockville, Md., 9 December 1982.

West Virginia. Department of Natural Resources. Division of Wildlife Resources. "Water Quality of Stony River and North Branch of Potomac River, Grant County." Interoffice Memorandum from Gerald E. Lewis and Virgil Ray to Eli McCoy, 8 November 1982. (Typewritten.)

West Virginia. Geological and Economic Survey. *Coal and Coal Mining in West Virginia,* by James A. Barlow. Coal Geology Bulletin no. 2. Morgantown, W. Va., February 1974.

West Virginia. Geological and Economic Survey. "A Cultural Resource Overview of the Monongahela National Forest. West Virginia." By R. P. Stephen Davis, Jr. Morgantown, W. Va., 1978.

West Virginia. Geological and Economic Survey. *Introduction to West Virginia Archeology.* By Edward V. McMichael. Educational Series, Morgantown, W. Va., 1963.

West Virginia. Geological Survey. *Geological Survey: Volume V, Forestry and Wood Industries.* By A.B. Brooks. Morgantown, W. Va.: The Acme Publishing Company, 1910.

West Virginia. Geological Survey. "The Romance of Coal," by James D. Sisler. Mimeograph Series I, Bulletin no. 3. Morgantown, W. Va., 1 April 1931.

West Virginia. Geological Survey. *West Virginia Geological Survey: Mineral and Grant Counties.* By David B. Reger, 1924.

West Virginia University. West Virginia Agricultural Experiment Station. Department of Agricultural Economics and Rural Sociology. *Elk Garden, West Virginia: A Reconnaissance Survey of a Problem Town.* By Ward F. Porter, Jr. Bulletin 355T, June 1952.

Whitman, Walt. *Passage to India.* New York: Haskell House Publishers Ltd., 1969.

Williams, Harold. *The Western Maryland Railway Story.* Baltimore: Western Maryland Railway Company, 1952.

Williams, John Alexander. "Davis and Elkins of West Virginia." Ph.D. dissertation, Yale University, 1967.

Wiseman, Roy. Elk Garden, West Virginia. Interviews, 10 May 1976, 10 November 1976, 11 March 1984.

Wright, Henry T., III. "A Preliminary Sequence for the Upper Potomac Valley." *The West Virginia Archeologist* 11 (September 1959): 9-21.

Index

Index

About the Author

GILBERT GUDE served in the U.S. House of Representatives (Eighth District, Maryland) from 1967 to 1976, and in the Maryland General Assembly for ten years before that. During his legislative service he build a record conspicuous for commitment to environmental protection and improvement. He was co-founder and co-chairman of the Environmental Study Conference, a key sponsor of the bill that created the C&O Canal Historical Park, and an unrelenting promoter of legislation associated with open space and parks, including a proposal to make the Potomac a national river. In 1975 he made a month-long fact-finding hike down the entire length of the Potomac. It was largely this experience that moved him to write *Where the Potomac Begins.*

Mr. Gude is a 1948 graduate in horticulture from Cornell University. He received an M.A. degree in public administration from George Washington University in 1958. Since 1977 he has been director of the Congressional Research Service at the Library of Congress. With a staff of 850, some 500 of whom are analysts, CRS provides reference information and custom-tailored research to members, committees, and staff of the U.S. Congress on a non-partisan basis. It ranks as the world's largest research organization in service to a legislative body.